Days Gone By

Days Gone By

in Contra
Costa County,
California

Volume 1

Nilda Rego

Contra Costa County Historical Society
Pleasant Hill, California

Days Gone By, Volume 1

Library Of Congress Catalog
Card Number 97–75218
ISBN: 1–889652–01–6

Contra Costa County Historical Society

Contents

The photographs on pages 183 and 187 are courtesy of the Wells Fargo History Room. The photograph on page 190 is courtesy of the Oakland Public Library, Oakland History Room. All other photographs are from the collection of the Contra Costa County Historical Society.

Preface

SO OFTEN we think of history in terms of cataclysmic events: wars, disasters, and pandemics. We learn dates, and the names of generals and presidents. This book is not that kind of history. Very few of the people in these stories would have made it onto the evening news. These are tales of ordinary people, sometimes doing extraordinary things, but mostly just trying to survive from day to day.

Since 1987, when I began writing local history, my resources have included numerous historic documents owned by the Contra Costa County Historical Society. I dedicate this volume to its volunteer staff, without whom the stories could not have been written.

Nilda Rego
Moraga, California
August 1997

Introduction

THE STORIES presented in this volume first appeared in the *Contra Costa Times*, published in Walnut Creek, California, in Nilda Rego's remarkably successful weekly column, "Days Gone By." Readers quickly became so completely addicted to her warm, homespun series of narratives relating the county's past that the editor of the *Times* was forced to print an explanation whenever Nilda's column did not appear as usual.

In 1991 the Conference of California Historical Societies, in recognition of Nilda's invaluable contribution to the preservation of local history, honored her with its prestigious Award of Merit.

Thanks to the cooperation of both the *Times* and Nilda Rego, the Contra Costa County Historical Society now makes available Volume One of a projected two-volume edition of "Days Gone By." Volume Two will be published in 1998.

Many staff members of the Contra Costa History Center devoted uncounted hours to preparing this book for publication. Most notably: June Whitesides, Bill and Tillie Larkins, Betty Maffei, and Bev Clemson.

Mary-Ellen Jones
President
Contra Costa County Historical Society

Opening of Carquinez Bridge

THE WEATHER during that week before Christmas 1926 turned out to be beautiful. Some people said it was almost balmy. Boaters were taking to the Carquinez Strait in big numbers.

"Many boatloads of sightseers have journeyed to the center of the stream to see the central tower, a piece of construction which is fast assuming shape. It is to act as the center piece of the bridge and will support seventy per cent of all the steel work, now in place," the *Contra Costa Gazette* reported on December 20.

"Two spans of approximately 320 feet each are being assembled for floating into place upon completion of the center span. According to (resident engineer George J.) Calder (it) will be the biggest job of its kind ever attempted on the Pacific Coast."

The bridge had been under construction since April 1923. But for those three years most of the work had been under water. The piers, each one as tall as an 11-story building were set in bedrock through 30-feet of sand, 135 feet below the surface of the water. "Old school" engineers had called the project impossible according to the *San Francisco Chronicle*. They said the current was too swift and too deep for the falsework needed to build the piers.

But the men who were masterminding the project were not engineers. Aven J. Hanford and Oscar Klatt had been in the grocery business before they started the Rodeo-Vallejo Ferry Co. in 1918. It was the ferry business that led them to bridge building.

Local interests were trying to finance the building of a bridge across the San Joaquin River from Antioch to Sherman Island. When it became apparent that they were going to fail Hanford and Klatt stepped into the breach. They organized the American Toll Bridge Co. and built the Victory Highway bridge for $3 million. Before the Antioch bridge was finished, the pair successfully sought the franchise to build a span across the Carquinez Strait, which was granted on February 5, 1923.

They hired Charles Derleth Jr., the dean of the engineering school at the University of California to be their chief engineer assisted by Calder. They planned a double cantilever bridge with two 1,100-foot spans and two 500-foot spans.

They tackled the swift current of the Strait by at first holding the piers in place with 120-foot steel piles hammered down 22 feet into the mud with their tops held down by eight-ton anchors and heavy chains.

In the early days of the bridge, planning money was scarce. Klatt and Hanford mortgaged their homes. Calder and Derleth kept designing and waited for their pay checks. Eventually Hanford and Klatt were able to put together a bond sale to finance the bridge, and the project moved ahead.

On Sunday October 3, 1926 the American Toll Bridge Co. invited representatives of the Bay Area press corps to lunch in Crockett and take a tour of the nearly-completed bridge. The invitation got them front page coverage in the *Contra Costa Gazette*.

"The entire party, comprising about three score, was then taken across the straits to the Solano shore where some of the more energetic climbed the 'golden stairs' (234 steps by actual count) . . . to the pierhead above Morrow Cover where Governor Richardson officiated last year at the pouring of the first concrete for the northern bridge terminal," reported the *Gazette* on the following Monday.

Derleth was the master of ceremonies. He told the newspaper men there were but "two bridges in the world larger than the cantilever Carquinez bridge, those being the Firth Bridge in Scotland and the Quebec Bridge in Canada, but as both are for railroad transportation only, the Carquinez bridge holds undisputed place as the greatest highway bridge in the world."

The *Gazette* printed the important statistics concerning the bridge including the fact that it would cost $8 million by the time it was complete. U.S. Steel Products had the contract for the structural steel; the United Brass Foundry of San Francisco cast the 3,000 fog warning bell, and the bond houses of Blyth, Witter & Co. of San Francisco, Houghtaling & Co. of Chicago, and Goodwin & Tucker of San Francisco financed the project.

Aven Hanford, president of the company, did not attend the gathering. He was represented by his brother, John, and Oscar

**Building the Carquinez Bridge, 1925. The view is from the Crockett side.
Note that the Solano shore is devoid of houses.**

Klatt. Hanford hadn't been feeling well. He had being feeling poorly for two years ever since he was in an auto accident on Tank Farm Hill near Crockett.

On October 26 Hanford was the speaker at the meeting of the San Francisco Secretaries Club at the Clift Hotel. He was back at his Berkeley home by 10 p.m. He complained of a headache and went to bed. By 9 a.m. Tuesday morning he was dead. He was 40 years old.

Klatt took over as president of the company. All work stopped on the bridge the day of Hanford's funeral in Berkeley, where it was announced that an urn containing Hanford's ashes "will be placed in a niche in the cornerstone of the Carquinez bridge. . . . A bronze plaque will also be placed there in honor of the builder."

At 2:30 p.m. on May 21, 1927 President Calvin Coolidge, seated in his office in the White House, pressed a golden key that activated a charge at the Carquinez bridge, which in turn provided the power to unfurl the American flag above the central tower of the bridge.

Hanford's widow climbed a decorated ladder and smashed a bottle of champagne on the superstructure of the bridge. The bottle had been one set aside by her husband. It was the last bottle of a case he bought in 1918 to commemorate the first ride on his and Klatz's ferry service.

More than 150,000 people attended the bridge opening on May 21. Mrs. Hanford was in the lead car across the bridge. The toll was 60 cents. The event was shoved off the front page of the *San Francisco Chronicle* by Charles Lindbergh's landing in Paris after his solo flight across the Atlantic.

Danville's First Developer

JOHN HARTZ didn't seem a likely candidate to become Danville's first developer in 1891.

He was a hard-working farmer who raised barley, wheat, and corn. He kept dairy cows, a few horses, chickens, and lots of pigs.

His wife, Catharina, helped in the fields and with the cows. Their children, Henry, Hannah, and Tillie, did their share of work. Tillie delivered milk to the townspeople door to door.

The couple spoke German in their home, reserving English for the outside world. Hartz didn't smoke, but his wife smoked cigars in the privacy of her home after daily chores were done, according to their grandson Duane Elliott, who still lives in Danville.

Hartz ran away from his home in northern Germany when he was 17 to avoid serving in the army. He arrived in New York in 1865, just as the Civil War was ending.

He had $10 left in his pockets by the time he reached California, so he took work as a farm hand in the Hayward area. During the next 10 years, he became a naturalized American citizen, married a girl from his boyhood village, and leased a farm in the Dublin area.

The family saved its money and by 1888 had enough to buy a farm. Hartz made the deal with Danville-area farmer James M. Stone, buying 220 acres for $27,500.

Two years later the railroad came to town and Hartz got into the subdivision business.

The Southern Pacific Co. paid Hartz $800 for 8.65 acres to lay tracks and build a station. However, the coming of the railroad split Hartz's farm, with 200 acres on one side of the tracks and less than 12 acres on the other.

The smaller parcel didn't make much sense for a farm that was mostly planted in wheat and barley, but it backed up against the strip of stores, a church, and a school that made up the community of Danville.

So Hartz hired civil engineer T. A. McMahon, a Martinez surveyor. They divided the land into 74 lots and Danville got its first subdivision.

Most of the lots were 50 feet wide by 100 feet in length. A few were 127 feet long. Hartz and McMahon crisscrossed the development with Hartz Avenue, School Street, Church Street, and two-block-long Short Street.

Hartz placed an ad in the *Contra Costa Gazette* on Aug. 19, 1891: "Lots for sale in the town of Danville on the line of the San Ramon Branch of the Southern Pacific Railroad formerly known as the J. M. Stone Tract. For further particulars enquire John Hartz, Danville."

Later that summer Hartz sold his first two lots. One went to Albert Flagel, a saloon keeper from Black Diamond, now Pittsburg.

The going price for the new lots was $150 each. Hartz accepted $10 down in gold coin. In some cases Hartz allowed the buyers to pay off the balance over a period of several years.

Danville in the early 1900s had a few stores, a church, and a lodge building shared by Grange members and the Oddfellows.

Edward McCauley bought four lots on Railroad Avenue, where he built the Danville Hotel.

Some of the lots were sold for homes. The Ramage family bought one and had a house built. When the head of the family died, in 1894, Hartz was called in to appraise the house and lot. It was valued at $750.

Widow Laura Ramage, who had been left with three young children, had a $300 mortgage. She couldn't make the payments.

The members of the Good Samaritan Club, Independent Order of Oddfellows Lodge 378, came to her rescue and put up $300 to prevent foreclosure.

Hartz was a lodge member in good standing in the Oddfellows. His wife cooked for the Oddfellows parties. After he retired from farming, in 1910, Hartz moved into town and took care of the maintenance and rentals at the Oddfellows Hall.

He still smoked his own meat, and Elliott remembers seeing crocks of salt pork in the cellar of the town house along with crocks of eggs preserved in clear gelatin.

Elliott, who was 11 years old when his grandfather died, remembers Hartz as a formal sort of person: "I never saw him in working clothes. He always wore a string tie."

Catharina Hartz and her daughter, Hannah, were also exceptional housekeepers.

On the day the two women scrubbed the floors of the house, John Hartz would have to leave. He usually would visit Tillie.

"They got that house shining. They wouldn't let him walk through his own front door. My mother thought that was terrible," Elliott said.

John Hartz wasn't beyond helping with the household chores. One day when he visited Tillie, she was canning.

"I remember him sitting in the kitchen peeling apricots," Elliott said.

Hartz also took his citizenship seriously, and voted whenever the opportunity arose.

In 1914 he was a registered Democrat. He told his daughter, "When the Democrats are in, we make more money."

He died in 1920. He was 73. He still owned a few of the lots he subdivided in 1891, and all his debts were paid.

The Houghs of Lafayette

ORLANDO HOUGH, a New Yorker, had been working long hours and earning little pay as a laborer. His jobs didn't pay much, at least not enough to support a wife. And he already had his eyes set on a young dark-haired school teacher, Emeline Bassett, in Gowanda, N.Y. His intentions were serious.

It must have been early in 1861 that he wrote his father, Sylvanus Hough, in California for advice.

Sylvanus Hough, 50, had been in California at least a year when Orlando's letter reached him. He was making $50 a month working on a cattle ranch owned by San Franciscan A. H. Houston, in what became Orinda. He had saved $750 towards buying cows to settle on his own place. His dream was to have his wife and only child, Orlando, join him as soon as he had earned enough money.

"You want me to give my advice about coming to Cal. I surtenly shal never give my advice to you or any other yong man to come to Calaforna unless thay will take it after thay git here. Their is thousands of yong men in this state that have bin here from two to ten years that can not git means to git to the Atlantick states and never will.

"If you or any other yong man come (to) Calaforna you must not think of giting ritch in short space of time. It is slow and shure that wins the race in Calaforna as well as in Newyork.

"If you think of going to the gold mines you had better stay at home and work for $10 per month. You will be better off ten years from now."

On the other hand, if Orlando wanted to bring his mother to California and then work with his father towards owning their own farm, Sylvanus thought the family could do pretty well.

"I think we could manage to git a living somehow without being slaves to other people. Callaforna is all sumer and no winter. We have about 6 months drouth in the year. We commence ploughing in Nov and fines [finish] in March anytime within the above menshend time will answer to put in crops. My buisness is over seeing a ranch and in rideing after cattle. I am the most of the time in the saddle. It will take 2 good horses to stand the rideing that I shal have to do the next 3 months."

Sylvanus's letter made up Orlando's mind. He proposed to Emma in December of 1861 and told her he was sailing to California. "I did not get that likeness of yours that you promised me. And in asking for youre likeness allow me also to ask you for the original, or in other words will you be mine," wrote Orlando.

Emma replied immediately.

"O you may have my likeness; and the 'other' which you spoke of, if you desire it above all others," she told her blue-eyed beau.

Orlando crossed the Isthmus of Panama in January of 1862, leaving Emma behind teaching in Gowanda. She was 23 and had been teaching since she was 14. It would be a year before she joined Orlando.

As soon as he arrived in Lafayette he wrote back to Emma.

"As for the journey to C why its nothing at all when you are once started. The sights which I saw paid me for all the trouble and expence. It would take 2 sheets of fools cap paper two tell you all that has transpired since I left New York."

Orlando ran a bigger risk and had more trouble getting to Lafayette from Oakland than he had on the whole trip, he told Emma. The eight-mile journey also cost him more mile per mile.

"It only cost me $10 for 2 horses to ride that 8 miles. You probably think as I did Emma, but after going over the road I thought it was very cheap."

By March of 1862 the Houghs had claimed a piece of land south of the Houston ranch, which would eventually extend for 1,000 acres.

Orlando ignored his father's advice and tried his hand at mining, but by July 1862 he could write Emma he was over his "mining fever." He also told her about the new business at his Lafayette ranch.

"I think cheese mining (is) about the best mining in Cal. as that article is in good demand at from 22 to 25 cts. per lb. We have now on hand about 140 good cheese (cheeses) which we intend to keep until fall."

In addition, Orlando was working with a reaping and threshing crew earning $52 a month.

The Civil War had been going on for 18 months when Orlando told Emma in August 1862 not to worry, he wasn't going to join up. Orlando said he wouldn't have hesitated to join the army if foreigners had invaded his country, but he didn't have it in him to fight his own countrymen.

Orlando didn't expect there would be many Army units from California joining in the struggle. They all would be too busy out west fighting Indians.

Late that October, Orlando suggested to Emma to include some warm clothing for her trip to California. "There is considerable cold here winters," he wrote.

The Hough house in Lafayette.

However, on that October day he told her the thermometer stood at 70 degrees in the shade.

"The ground is as dry as a bone and the wild roses continue to bud and blow though it was only spring."

In a Jan. 23, 1863 letter Orlando mentioned a visitor at the Lafayette ranch.

"We have had quite an interesting visitor stopping to our house for several days. He is from Missouri and was taken prisoner by the rebels gurillas and detained 5 months. He tells some verry hard stories about rebeldome."

In the same letter Orlando said, "I cant make it seem at all like winter here. It is very warm & pleasant today. Not a cloud in sight. It seems more like June than Jan. By the time you arrive the hills & vallies will be covered with flowers of all coulors. Wont we have a nice time Emma."

The price of cheese in the meanwhile had dropped in 1863 and Orlando worried about profits.

"I expect we shal commence making cheese next month. We calculate to milk 100 or 115 cows this year. If cotton cloth keeps up to the present price it will cost nearly 60 cents to bandage a cheese weighing 30 lbs or 2 cts per pound for bandage cloth. Cheese is worth from 15 to 18 cts per lb."

On Jan. 24, 1863 Orlando sent Emma a $200 draft to be drawn on Wells, Fargo for her passage to California via the Isthmus of Panama.

Even after they were married the Houghs continued to write letters whenever they were separated. These letters detail life in Lafayette from the 1860s through the 1880s. The Houghs, who had four children, wrote about everything that happened in their little town from disastrous events such as losing parts of their rancho to land speculator Horace Carpentier to taking buckets of honey out of a bee tree.

Oil Wells in Orinda

IF JAMES MINER could have made a better living farming off his 612 acres in Orinda, he never would have given the greasy liquid he found seeping up on his property a second look.

But he had three daughters to raise. That took money.

The Miner family had been living in Orinda ever since 1879 when Miner's Uncle Solomon Alden bought the property as an investment. Miner improved an existing house on the property, moved his family into it and started raising horses, hay, grain, and vegetables.

The land was bordered by a little creek, and whenever Miner's horses trod in the soft dirt by the stream their hoofprints filled with a peculiar brown liquid. He scooped up some of the fluid, put it in a tin can, and forgot about it.

After 16 years struggling with declining prices, uncertain weather, and the Orinda soil, Miner became convinced there had to be a better way to make a living then farming. It was then he took a second look at the stuff he had put in the tin can years before. The liquid had become stickier and waxy. It definitely smelled like tar.

Miner invited some oil experts to come to his farm. They pronounced the substance a "splendid article of petroleum," according to an 1895 article in the *San Francisco Chronicle*.

"Thus encouraged the rancher began a series of experiments. He drove the point of an iron rod into the soft earth, and in almost every instance gas escaped from the hole.

"Pursuing his investigation, he turned his attention to the bed of a little mountain stream which is noisy in its rush through the green meadows of the tract. There he found a ledge of shale tipping abruptly to the southeast. The whack of a pick disturbed big pieces of stone, and where they fell into the stream the water became iridescent with oil. The basins he dug on the shore soon filled with water, and upon the surface there quickly floated bits of a substance as brown as tobacco-juice. These brown splashes were coal oil of the heaviest character.

"Half a mile from the spot in the creek where he first sank his pick the rancher discovered a spring in a sandstone formation which was covered with oil. He sank an iron rod into the pool, and when he withdrew it the water began to boil violently.

"A blazing match placed above the troubled spot produced a greater flame, and as the water boiled its surface was covered with oil."

The *Chronicle* had no doubt that there was oil under Miner's ranch and that the discovery could lead to a field where there was so much oil it could solve "the fuel question on the coast."

The paper quoted A. L. McPherson of Oakland, who was said to have opened up oil fields in Southern California.

"If money can be raised to sink a well or two, I am sure the people of Central California at least will be relieved of the excessive rates now charged by the oil trust and its lusty twin, the Southern Pacific Railroad Company. . . . I know it could be

The oil derrick at Camp Miner.

pumped to Oakland for 2 cents a barrel. Where manufacturers are now paying $7 and $9 a ton for fuel they could get the same results for one-third the money," said McPherson.

McPherson wasn't an innocent bystander. He was trying to get investors to develop an oil well on the Miner property.

The Miner ranch wasn't the only spot in the county where oil prospecting was going on. As far back as 1865, 62 petroleum companies were incorporated in California; seven of these were in Contra Costa. Oil had been reported in Pacheco, the San Pablo Valley, and east of Mount Diablo.

On March 4, 1865 the *Contra Costa Gazette* reported the discovery of oil.

"The report of the finding of petroleum springs in our county has been pretty generally circulated. As far as we have been able to learn, the truth is as follows: A large extent of the country has been taken up by claimants just east of Mt. Diablo, and a couple of miles south of the Pittsburg and neighboring coal mines. In this vicinity one company has been engaged in boring for some time, and another has just begun. It is the Adams Company that has been busy boring for some time; after boring some 150 or more feet, water and oil commenced flowing out together, there being about three quarters of an inch of oil on the surface of the water as it came pouring out."

In July 1865 the *Gazette* reported the Adams Petroleum Company "has struck oil in their new well in such quantity to indicate beyond doubt an inexhaustible supply."

While the Adams well didn't prove to be the bonanza first predicted, in February of 1900 another company, The Contra Costa Oil and Petroleum Company, acquired the same land and started drilling all over again.

Meanwhile, back at Miner's ranch, prospecting for oil continued. One well reached the depth of 1,500 feet when the drill broke off and couldn't be recovered, remembered Miner's daughter, Anita, many years later.

Then on Oct. 17, 1903 the *Call* of San Francisco reported the gusher for which everyone had been waiting for so long at the Miner ranch.

"Oil that has been sought for by an enterprising company for years was discovered last Wednesday evening on the Miner ranch, and as the murky fluid shot up into the air it suddenly became ignited. The column of flame could be seen for miles and presented a magnificent sight. Many workmen in the vicinity had barely time to escape with their lives and much machinery was entirely destroyed by the flames. the oil became ignited by several lanterns that hung on a derrick at the side of the well."

The American Oil and Refining Company had been boring wells on the Miner ranch for four years when the well blew and all the equipment was lost. Miner died six years later and the family moved to Oakland. But oil prospecting didn't stop.

In 1929 the Orinda Petroleum Company built a 122-foot derrick and bored a 3,033-foot hole. Two years and $100,000 later the company called it quits and in 1939 the derrick was dynamited and removed because of its hazard to the community.

That still isn't the end of the story. In 1969, when the BART tunnel was being built from Orinda through the Berkeley Hills into Oakland, oil was found again. Spokesmen for the contractor reported minor oil seeps on the Orinda side, which were not expected to cause any tunneling trouble.

Anything Grows

EARLY FARMERS AND RANCHERS in Contra Costa County were so amazed at the climate compared to what they had back east, they were ready to plant anything from banana plants to tobacco.

In fact, in 1874 Dr. John Strenzel displayed his grapes at the Contra Costa County Fair around a banana plant, no doubt grown at his farm in Martinez. A year later a group of growers tried to start a tobacco plantation in Pacheco.

Dr. J. H. Carothers, the founder of Pacheco, leased 70 acres of his land to the Pacheco Tobacco Company, and during the last week in April of 1875 the editor of the *Contra Costa Gazette* dropped by to see what was happening.

"We found the work of ridging and setting the plants in active progress under the direction of Mr. Cornell, the superintendent. Some six or more teams were employed in the various operations of plowing, ridging, etc., and about twenty Chinamen in setting and (inserting) shields covering the plants."

By the end of July a "vigorous and handsome stand of plants" were reported to be growing in Carothers' field. However, instead of the 70 acres first planned, the crop had been cut back to 35 acres. Samples of the tobacco leaves were sent to experts for analysis, who said the leaves showed the Pacheco crop to be "the best conditioned" of the year.

A successful tobacco crop could earn quite a bit of money. It cost $100 an acre to grow and cure the tobacco and the returns could range from $500 to $1,000 an acre. This was remarkable profit when farmers growing wheat netted $10 per acre.

However, tobacco was not to be the bonanza crop for Pacheco. It was an experiment that lasted one year. Contra Costa's climate was not hot enough to grow the leaf.

Perhaps Contra Costa would be the land of the olive. Olive trees had been planted in Contra Costa since the days of the Spanish rancheros, but it took a glove manufacturer from San

Francisco to start an olive oil manufacturing plant here in the 1880s.

Fred Busby chose 104 acres between Clayton and Concord to plant his olive grove. He installed great stone wheels to press the olives and opened a bottling plant. Within a few years he was winning prizes for his olive oil at the California State Fair.

The 1882 map and brochure of Contra Costa County printed by the Elliott Publishing Co. of San Francisco described Busby's olive oil as "second to none. . . . His oil possesses that delicacy of flavor not found in oil produced outside of mountain districts, while his ripe and green pickled olives are a luxury that all epicures are familiar with."

Apparently Busby made more money in the glove business than in the olive oil business. After the 1906 earthquake, he moved his San Francisco glove manufacturing plant to Oakland and little more was heard about his olive oil. Other farmers continued to cultivate the olive tree in and about Concord. In 1911

**Contra Costa's display at the 1932 California State Fair—
a cornucopia of riches in a Roman setting.**

Peter Magini tried to start the Mt. Diablo Olive Oil and Canning Co., to be headquartered in Concord. His dream was to handle all the olives grown in the area and turn them either into oil or soap. His Concord dream came to naught. After a few newspaper articles, his company was never heard from again.

Busby's original olive orchard was pulled up in 1929 to clear the acreage for a truck farm. By the 1920s irrigation had entered the Contra Costa farm picture. More and more growers dug wells, installed pumps, and gave up dry farming for irrigated acres.

By 1910 Contra Costa ranked second of all the 58 counties in the state in the production of almonds, second in potato production, third in all vegetables, fifth in hay and forage, 12th in milk products, 13th in barley products, and 14th in all cereal products.

There was no doubt about it. In 1910 Contra Costa was farm country. Of its 456,950 acres, 406,000 were designated as farm land by the Secretary of State in the California Blue Book.

If Contra Costa continued to be the agricultural power it started out to be, perhaps the tomato would have been its reigning crop. The red fruit started becoming popular with growers around 1911 when a group of cannery owners in Antioch who were putting up celery began looking around for another crop to can. They came into Concord to try to convince a few farmers to raise tomatoes. What they needed to keep their cannery going after the celery season was 200 acres of tomato plants.

"Ten to 20 tons to the acre is the average yield and the pay is proposed to be at the rate of $7 a ton, the grower to furnish his own boxes. The picking and loading will cost about $1 a ton," reported the *Concord Transcript.*

By the 1930s the tomato became such a popular crop in the area in and about Concord that a cannery was constructed in Walnut Creek.

"The Walnut Creek Cannery is operating at practically full capacity, according to R. C. Franke, owner. Seventeen women and sixteen men, all local people are employed at present and a larger force will be employed later when the run of tomatoes increases.

"Franke will pack 2,500 tons of locally grown tomatoes, which are unusually good this year, he said. Most of this output is for eastern markets, with the exception of three carloads of tomato catsup which will be shipped to England. Catsup and puree are the only two commodities that he will pack,"reported the *Walnut Creek Courier Journal* in the summer of 1937.

Giving the tomato a run for its money were pears, apricots, walnuts, almonds, grapes, peaches, and even cauliflower.

Ygnacio Valley in 1923 was becoming famous for its cauliflower crop according to the *Concord Transcript*.

"Meinert Station near here is this week shipping to the eastern markets its first crop of cauliflower. There are in all about 25 cars of the vegetable billed out over the San Francisco and Sacramento Railroad. The entire crop is bound for points east of the Mississippi."

In the 1930s and 1940s Contra Costa County's display at the state fair featured boxes and baskets of fruits and vegetables grown. The county's industries only took up small corners of the display. But already the curtain was coming down on Contra Costa's leading agricultural role in the state. The Caldecott Tunnel was completed in 1937 and the subdivisions of the vineyards, wheat fields, walnut and olive orchards had begun.

The Birth of Alameda County

NATIVE CALIFORNIAN Mariano Guadalupe Vallejo got the job at the Constitutional Convention in 1850 to divide the state into counties. His committee found it a tough job.

There were no accurate maps. The baseline on Mount Diablo from which all land measurements were to flow had yet to be established. Boundary markers were rivers, mountain ridges, prominent ranchos, rocks, or even trees.

Legal documents describing property limits were full of references such as "two miles south of (Robert) Livermore's rancho" or "opposite the dividing ridge between Taylor's valley and the residence of Widow Welch."

Vallejo's committee settled on 27 counties. He would have preferred the name of Mount Diablo for what became known as Contra Costa County.

"It was intended so to call the county (Mount Diablo), but both branches of the Legislature, after warm debates on the subject resolved upon the less profane one (name) of Contra Costa," Vallejo wrote.

Contra Costa was about twice its present size. It included all the land west of the Oakland-Berkeley hills reaching as far south as Alameda Creek, the boundary line now separating Hayward and Fremont.

On the east side of the hills the Contra Costa line followed the San Joaquin River turning west near the source of Alameda Creek (Niles Canyon) and included the area that became Dublin. Contra Costa's southern next door neighbor was Santa Clara County.

Martinez too far from Oakland

The first thing that Contra Costa County had to do after being formed was to divide itself into three townships—New York (Antioch), Martinez, and San Antonio (Oakland.) The Martinez township reached from the Suisun Straits to two miles south of Livermore's rancho.

Three townships for the 722 people who lived in Contra Costa at the time seemed about right until one considered the distances to be traveled. It wasn't long before the three townships became seven. But this still wasn't satisfactory. Martinez was at the northern end of a very long county. To do any county business people in Oakland had to travel more than 30 miles, using the hazardous trails across the mountain ridges separating the east part of the county from the west.

In 1852 the community of Oakland started proceedings for incorporation. Pushing the little town into city status was one Horace W. Carpentier, a young attorney from the east. It didn't bother him one bit that the land he was claiming belonged to the distinguished Peralta family.

Carpentier had no doubts that Oakland was the spot to be in the coming years. He had already petitioned the Contra Costa County government officials to start a ferry from San Antonio (East Oakland) to San Francisco.

He paid a license fee of $10 and put up a $1,000 bond in Martinez for the privilege of ferrying passengers across the bay. He was to provide daily service and could charge $1 per passenger, $3 per horse, and $5 per horse and wagon.

More votes than voters in Oakland

San Antonio, located on El Camino Real (the King's Highway), was the point where stages arrived from Concord, Pleasanton, Alvarado, Stockton, and San Jose to go to San Francisco. It was the place that farmers brought their produce, and where pack trains headed for the gold country loaded on supplies to take to the mines. While Oakland was struggling to be incorporated, the whole of what was then southern Contra Costa County was working on separation.

Carpentier thought he could control both issues by being elected to the legislature. However, H. C. Smith of Alvarado, who represented Contra Costa County in 1852, submitted the petition to incorporate Oakland before the election. Carpentier had a second agenda. Not only did he want southern Contra Costa to be its own county, he wanted Oakland to be the county seat. So still seeing a lot of benefits by being in the legislature, Carpentier tossed his hat into the ring in 1853.

An old monument from the county line between
Alameda and Contra Costa counties, 1896.

Running against him was B. R. Holliday, Martinez's first school teacher, who had served the county as both coroner and justice of the peace, and Robert S. Farrelly of Squattersville (San Lorenzo.) Carpentier didn't care how he won as long as he won. When the votes were counted he had 519. Farrelly had 254 and Holliday 192. There was one big problem with the vote. Too many ballots were cast. Farrelly cried "fraud" and hired S. J. Clark as his attorney. Carpentier was denied his seat while the matter was investigated by the legislature's Committee on Elections.

Alameda County is Born

Clark charged the board of judges, the inspectors and clerks of Contra Costa, and the township of Oakland with collusion.

He showed that the whole of the Oakland township had 130 eligible voters, while 373 people voted there. In addition, he showed that on election day a stack of ballots, all for Carpentier, were found in a compact package on top of the ballot box. Clark also found a witness, a Mr. Ford, who happened to use Carpentier's ferry on election day.

Ford signed an affidavit, which stated that while on the ferry he saw one T. C. Gilman buy ferry tickets for 37 men. Ford recognized these men at the polls and overheard one of them say he had voted seven times.

The Contra Costa Board of Supervisors presented its own affidavit. It favored Carpentier.

The state election committee stated that there was no cause to wonder at the large vote for Carpentier because it was only 66 more than was found to reside in the district the previous August.

"And the fact that there were 300 to 400 persons in the Redwoods and most of them voted in Oakland left no doubt that the votes were honestly cast by qualified electors," the committee reported.

Carpentier was seated, but in the meantime the legislature had convened in Benicia. Smith presented the petition creating Alameda County by carving out portions of Contra Costa and Santa Clara counties, beating Carpentier again. Carpentier was seated in the Assembly just in time to join the fight over where to put the county seat.

Carpentier lobbied for Oakland. Smith plugged for his hometown of Alvarado and he won by two votes.

Contra Costa worth half of Alameda

The division left Contra Costa County with an evaluation of $2,330,084 and Santa Clara with $6,583,062. The new county of Alameda was worth $4,383,179.

"The division gave dissatisfaction in Santa Clara and Contra Costa Counties as was to be expected," wrote William Halley in his *Centennial Yearbook of Alameda County,* published in 1876.

Some former Contra Costa residents sent a memorial to the legislature protesting their inclusion in the new Alameda County. Some residents of San Pablo wanted to form their own county, separating from what was left of Contra Costa. Still others in Contra Costa were so dissatisfied they got Carpentier to introduce a bill to get back some of the territory taken by Alameda County. But the legislature didn't change its mind. Contra Costa kept its name (meaning the opposite coast), but it did lose most of its East Bay shoreline. The other thing Contra Costa got to keep was a $7,400 debt for an unfinished bridge in Alameda County.

Nancy Joins the WCTU

FRANCIS (FRANK) MARION YAGER was known to take a nip now and then. It was a habit his wife, Nancy Alice Foster Yager, tried to break. She was a stalwart member of the Women's Christian Temperance Union.

The Yagers lived in Alamo around the turn of the century with their 13 daughters, Birdie, Elfleda, Maud, Susan, Frances, Mary, Daisy, Bell, Alda, Ruth Cleveland, Bessie, Margarite, and Norma. On shopping day Frank would load his wife and daughters into the bed of the wagon, hitch up the horse, and go off to Walnut Creek.

While Alice was buying groceries Frank would head for the nearest saloon to meet his friends.

On a particular day that all the daughters seemed to remember in later years, Frank had had a little too much to drink.

Bernice Strutton of Antioch remembers the story her mother, Ruth Cleveland Yager ("Grandpa was a Democrat") told her. Ruth was the 10th daughter.

"Grandma went to pick grandpa up at the saloon. He was in a very happy mood and wanted to kiss her. He kept trying to tease her, grab her. She threw a potato at him. And he threw it back."

The potato throwing contest went on all the way back to Alamo. Not only wouldn't Nancy Alice let her husband drive the wagon, she wouldn't let him climb into it.

"Mother said she would never forget him throwing the potatoes back. He walked all the way home behind the wagon."

The Yagers arrive in 1850

Frank, a native of Missouri, had come to California with his widowed father, two brothers, and two sisters when he was nine years old in 1850. Cornelius Yager was a traveling Presbyterian minister who had made plans with his wife, Susan Berry, to cross the plains in 1849. But Susan died and Cornelius had to make the trip without her.

The WCTU in Concord, during a dry spell.

In 1851 Cornelius bought a share of the Romero Rancho in Alamo with three partners. He moved on to the property with his married daughter, Sarah Caldwell, and his other four children. It was there under Sarah's watchful eye that Frank grew up.

Cornelius Yager had barely settled in Contra Costa when he was elected County Clerk. In 1860 he was sent to the legislature. He preached throughout the mining communities of California, and when he died in Fresno in 1895 his obituary appeared in numerous newspapers all over the state.

The *Fresno Republican* reported: "He was temperate in all things, and noted for steadfast devotion of mission work that took no note of physical weariness or alterations of heat and cold. He was always at his post, wherever his duty called him. He mostly traveled in a buggy through the foothills, but his erect, stalwart form might quite as often be seen striding over the country as if fatigue were a thing unknown long after he passed his 70th year."

Sisters disapprove of Frank's wife

Shirley MacFarland of Napa, another granddaughter of the Yagers, said that her mother, Daisy (the 7th daughter), told her that Cornelius probably introduced his son Frank to his future wife, Nancy Alice Foster. The preacher had met the Foster family while he was working in the Gold Country. The friendship continued when the Fosters moved to San Francisco.

Frank and Alice were married in 1875. Frank may have been married, but he was a hard man to stay put.

"He would move her into a house and go off on a job," said his granddaughter, Jacqueline Bryan, of Paso Robles. "Frank was the typical black sheep of the family."

The Yagers' granddaughters didn't know anything about the courtship of Frank and Nancy Alice. But Bryan, whose mother, Norma, was the youngest of the girls, said that Frank's sisters didn't approve of Frank's wife.

"They (the sisters) thought he had married beneath him until they realized that she was raising the girls and doing a good job of it." Nancy Alice Foster Yager was born in northern California, probably around Foster's Bar. Her parents were William and Sarah Foster, who had survived the terrible tragedy of the Donner Party.

Frank invents a washing machine

Nancy Alice and Frank had a good marriage. Nancy Alice apparently was the most patient of women. Her husband was a farmer, a tinkerer, and a dreamer. Once in a while he made something that helped Alice out. He invented a washing machine, which took two of his daughters to operate. It probably didn't work all that well because there is also a family story about washing clothes in a creek near Alamo.

"One of the sisters was down at the creek washing clothes with a board. She looked up and across the stream and saw a mountain lion staring at her. She threw the wash board at it. It ran away. And she kept on washing," said MacFarland.

All three granddaughters remember their mothers telling them that Nancy Alice was a superb housekeeper.

"Mother said she could see herself in the silver (trimming) on the stove. She (Nancy Alice) used ashes from the fire to keep the silver part clean," said Strutton.

Nancy Alice was also a very frugal housekeeper. She had to be with 13 daughters to raise.

"Grandmother made curtains out of sugar sacks. She embroidered them. Most of the girls' dresses were made of sugar sacks. She'd bleach them. She was a very neat, clean lady," said Strutton.

Underwear out of sugar sacks

MacFarland's mother, Daisy, told her that Nancy Alice also sewed all their underwear out of sugar sacks.

"One day Bessie (the 11th daughter) fell down, showing her bloomers. Across the rear of her pants was printed 'Our Family's Pride,'" said MacFarland.

As the 13 daughters grew up they took over many of their mother's chores. Susan, the fourth born, became the dressmaker. She sewed the wedding dresses for her nieces. Each girl had to do her own washing and ironing and each one had a cubicle for her clothes. All the garments were labeled. Once a week the whole house was scrubbed down including the windows.

The Yagers continued to be strong Presbyterians throughout their married life. Even though Frank was a bit of a wanderer, when he was home he read the Bible to his daughters every night.

"My mother (Ruth) knew the Bible backwards," said Strutton.

"Christmas was the big holiday. Grandma would start making dolls in June. She'd buy the dolls' heads and make the bodies. They would cut a (Christmas) tree from the property, get tin cans, paint them different colors, and hang them on the trees. The candles were lit on Christmas Eve."

Everyone in the family was expected to perform on Christmas. Strutton's mother was the dancer. Some would recite.

"Each one had some talent that Grandma tried to bring out."

When he wasn't inventing things, Frank was dreaming about the fabled family inheritance. Just before Cornelius died he proved he was in line to inherit a $50,000 fortune in Germany through his grandmother, Elizabeth Fisher. The money was in the Bank of Hamburg awaiting settlement. After his father's death, in 1895, Frank began working on the estate. However, he too died before any settlement was made, and then came World War I and the inheritance disappeared.

Frank died in 1908 in Willows, where he had found the last of his many jobs. Nancy Alice then married an old Alamo neighbor, Josiah Smith.

The Mystery of Sam Bacon

THE FOLKS in and about Concord didn't seem at all surprised when Sam Bacon, the town's first postmaster, died on Jan. 7, 1891.

As the *Contra Costa Gazette* put it, "His health was never rugged and with advancing age his infirmities increased until his system gradually gave way." He was 57 years old.

Whatever did Bacon in wasn't clear. His right hand had been shaking for so long that he had taken to writing with his left. Sometimes his arm would ache because of that shaking. Both Dr. Edmond Bragdon and Dr. Francis Neff handled his medical care primarily by injecting him with morphine to "quiet him."

Bacon died on a Tuesday and was buried at the Oddfellows Cemetery in Pacheco on Sunday. By the middle of February his family was squabbling over his substantial estate, reputed to be around $40,000.

Three of his seven children sought to break Bacon's will, charging that their stepmother forced their father to short-change them in the matter of Bacon's estate.

Bacon seeks California gold

Bacon had made his fortune by lending money, buying and selling land, and operating Concord's first general store. He was born and educated in Barre, Mass. In 1851, when he was 18, he decided to seek his fortune in the California gold mines. He bought a ticket on a stage coach to Illinois and then hitched a ride with a friend who was driving an ox team to Iowa. At Council Bluffs he joined a wagon train of 138 people, which was headed to California via Fort Bridger and Salt Lake.

After a year trying to grub a living in the mines, he left the gold country and came down to Contra Costa County. He got a job building stables for 14 Army mules at the Government Ranch near Concord. In 1855 Bacon was able to claim a piece of land for himself, a quarter section at Bay Point (Port Chicago). By the time five more years had gone by, Bacon knew two more things about himself. He was neither a miner nor a farmer.

So in 1860 he opened up a fruit and stationery store in Pacheco, which didn't turn out to be such a good idea either. Not that he wasn't cut out to be a merchant. It was just that he picked a town that was plagued by floods. Downtown Pacheco, the fastest growing community in Contra Costa in 1860, kept getting inundated every rainy season, and Bacon's writing pads and printed forms kept getting wet.

Bacon buys Concord city lot for $1

The flooding problem was so bad that Don Salvio Pacheco, his son Fernando, and his son-in-law Francisco Galindo, three of the area's biggest landowners, came up with a solution. They would start a new town on 20 acres, further east and a little to the south. And they'd call it Todos Santos. The three hired Luis Castro, Alameda County surveyor, to draw up a plan of the new town. Then to each of the flood victims of Pacheco they offered a city lot for $1.

Bacon was the first to take up the offer. He built a new store, and this time decided to expand his business by selling all types of merchandise including tobacco. Bacon came up with the idea to improve business by offering a three-percent discount to his customers who paid cash. He also lent money, charging 10 percent per year interest.

The little town prospered, and by 1869 changed its name to Concord. By 1872 it was decided that Concord needed a post

**The Bacon children posed outside their house,
next to Bacon's general store (far left), in the 1870s.**

office, and where better to put it than in a corner of Bacon's general store.

Bacon was appointed postmaster, a job which he kept for the next 14 years. Sooner or later everyone in Concord came to Bacon's store to pick up or post their letters, and the post office became the town's unofficial meeting place. At the same time Bacon got the post office job he was licensed as a notary public, and then became the Wells Fargo Express and insurance agent. In 1873 he became Concord's first justice of the peace.

Children cut out of estate

Bacon's first wife, the mother of his seven children, died during this period of prosperity. In September 1874 he married his second wife, Marietta Norton. At the time, his youngest daughter, Clara, was 6 years old.

About a month before he died, Bacon made out a new will leaving all of his estate to Marietta except for a $300 bequest to each of his seven children, who were all adults.

The three eldest, William, Sarah, and Annie, sued to overturn the will, contending that their father was not in his right mind and had been unduly influenced by his wife. They said that Bacon's health started going downhill after his marriage to Marietta.

Sarah Bacon Latimer, 33, testified that she first saw her father take opium in 1878.

"He took it in powders and bought it in drachm bottles. I have seen him take the opium on a pen knife, put it in a spoon and then inject the same into his arm or leg by a syringe, which he had for that purpose.

"In the year 1878, following my marriage, early one evening my sisters came running down from my father's house to where I was living with my husband. They were greatly excited and said father was dying. I immediately went down to his residence and found him lying on a bed. He was in an unconscious condition. We at once called a physician for him and the physician told us he had taken too much opium and treated him for the same. (He) directed me to give father strong coffee to work off the effect of the drug."

Bacon was a drug addict

The three eldest children said that their father had a stroke in 1884 as a result of using excessive amounts of alcohol, morphine, opium, and other drugs, and his judgement had been impaired.

Sarah said that when her father's body was being prepared for the coffin, her stepmother boasted, "Your father has made his will and what is more none of you can break it."

Henry Tillman, Bacon's son-in-law and business partner, was the star witness for Marietta. Tillman had been accused by the three eldest children of having been given Bacon's share of the business a month before he died, and that it was worth $10,000. Tillman testified that he bought Bacon's share of the store, and produced the company's books to back his statements.

Tillman said that he and his wife, Florence, lived with Sam and Marietta Bacon and that they never saw him under the influence of liquor or drugs.

"As far as I know his mental condition was perfect," said Tillman. He admitted that he saw Bacon's doctors inject him with morphine, but insisted that his (Bacon's) mind was clear. Marietta denied the allegations put forth by the three children.

Judge Joseph Jones's instructions to the jury included the observation that only three of Bacon's seven children were suing to break the will. He added that even if Bacon was in the habit of using morphine or any other drug, that fact alone wouldn't be sufficient to overturn the will.

Was Bacon in his right mind?

The jury also would have to find "That the use of such morphine or other drug had so impaired the intellect of the decedent S. Bacon, that he did not have mental capacity to execute a will, because a man may have used drugs of the character indicated and still have complete possession of his mental faculties," said the judge.

The trial took four days. The jury deliberated for more than six hours and in the end sustained the will. The judge ordered the plaintiffs to pay Marietta's court costs. The plaintiffs promised not to appeal the verdict if Marietta forgave the court costs. She agreed.

The Great Balloon Disaster

THE WEATHER had been rather warm that week preceding the Fourth of July in 1889 and there was no reason to think it was about to change.

The proprietor of the Alhambra Hotel was banking on a hot afternoon. He had erected a tent in front of his establishment. He asked Mrs. D. Rowell to sell her homemade ice cream and lemonade to the crowd that was sure to gather after the annual parade.

W. K. Coles, who owned the drug store on Main Street, was also planning a special ice cream confection. He hoped the hot weather would send people into his establishment to try out his new ice cream sodas.

The organizers of Martinez's Fourth of July festivities had managed a coup. For the first time in county history there would be a balloon ascension on this side of the Oakland-Berkeley hills. The Fourth of July committee, which included the most important businessmen in town—Simon Blum, L. M. Lasell, I. Weiss, S. J. Perry, and E. W. Hiller—had hired a balloonist, Prof. Frank Munroe.

It had been a busy week for Blum. The steam schooner *Cosmopolis* from Coos Bay Harbor had arrived with 300,000 feet of lumber. He had spent most of Tuesday, July 2, down at Granger's Wharf seeing to the unloading.

Balloonist to get $150

All five members of the committee had their fingers crossed. They hoped the afternoon breeze wouldn't fail them. Munroe, the experienced aeronaut of San Francisco, would get $150 if the ascension was a success. If the weather turned foul and he couldn't get off the ground he was assured of $75 for his trouble in bringing his balloon to Martinez.

People had been paying 25 cents to get into Woodward's Gardens and Central Park in the city across the Bay to see the professor ascend in this balloon. It was 55 by 40 feet and was expected to reach heights of from 1,000 to 3,000 feet. Munroe was to arrive two days before the Fourth to search out the best spot to inflate the balloon and make the ascension.

The committee also spent more than $300 on fireworks. An American eagle in brilliant colored lace work was to be lit up, along with an exhibition scroll wheel. There would be 48 one- and two-pound skyrockets, 12 Japanese bombs that would be fired from two mortars 200 feet into the sky, and six Boyton report rockets that were said to make a boom as loud as a six-pound cannon.

Professor Munroe chose Seely Bennett's empty lot to inflate his balloon. Bennett owned the livery stable on Ferry Street and operated the stage that made trips up to Mount Diablo.

On Thursday, July 4, people in Martinez awoke to brilliant sunshine. There was a breeze blowing off the straits. People had come by train and buggy from all over the county to see the parade, the fireworks, and, of course, Professor Munroe.

Crowd gathers to watch balloonist

The parade started at 10:30 a.m., going up Ferry Street to Main and then back and forth until all the little streets in downtown Martinez had their view of the marchers.

The Martinez Brass Band led the parade and was immediately followed by the "Car of State."

"Forty-two young girls, appropriately costumed, representing every State in the Union, their fresh and happy faces glowing with pleasure and the excitement naturally inspired by the occasion, with the Goddess of Liberty, Miss Mary Smith, in the centre," reported the *Contra Costa Gazette* on July 6.

After the parade the crowd went over to the opera house to hear the band and the town glee club perform patriotic pieces. Mary Bertola read the Declaration of Independence and Gen. G. W. Bowie gave the oration of the day.

Professor Monroe was the next event on the day's calendar, but by now the breeze off the strait was blowing briskly. The crowd milled around Bennett's lot, watching the professor struggling for half an hour to inflate the balloon. The professor then announced that he was going to wait another hour, hoping the wind would be more cooperative.

The crowd went down to the Commercial Hotel on Main Street to watch the race for men 50 years and older. It was won by Michael McNamara, who took home a box of cigars.

Amy Nelson won a gold ring for coming in first in the girls' race, and William Peralta caught the greased pig, which he got to keep. The married men beat the single men in the tug of war and got to share in a box of cigars.

It was midafternoon by the time the aeronaut was ready to try his balloon ascension.

Smoke pours out on crowd

The *Contra Costa Gazette* described the event in its Saturday issue.

"The eager crowd once more gathered at the appointed spot to witness the novel sight. The fire was started under the balloon and the huge bag began to assume shape.

"A number of firemen were delegated to assist in the inflation,

Crowds lined Main Street in Martinez to see the Goddess of Liberty in the 1889 Fourth of July parade.

and as the balloon gracefully swayed in the breeze, under the pressure of the hot air, it presented a grand sight and all anxiously awaited the moment for it to ascend heavenward.

"At last the word was given, the band struck up, and the aeronaut in gay colored tights grasped the bar, the rope was cast off and the balloon started, but instead of ascending into the blue vault of the heavens as was expected, dragged along the ground in the direction of the Gazette office, where it became wedged between the trees and the fence, dragging the aeronaut against the same, scratching his hands and face quite badly, where it turned over on its side and was badly torn by coming in contact with the fence, while the hot air and smoke, with which it was inflated, poured out in volumes upon the crowd."

The accident ended the balloon ascension for the day. Munroe blamed the disaster on the weather, but the editor of the *Gazette* thought otherwise.

"It is the opinion of many who watched closely the maneuvers of Prof. Munroe and his assistants during that afternoon, that it was not his intention to make an ascension at all. The balloon was certainly not more than half inflated, and had it succeeded in passing the trees would not have gone up more than a hundred feet at the most, and from all appearances, it was unable to lift itself from the ground. . . . It was a great disappointment to all, and as many believe that it was a fake, considerable dissatisfaction prevails."

The Fourth of July committee reluctantly paid Munroe $75 for his trouble. The crowd went back to Main Street to watch the drill of the Martinez Hook and Ladder Company.

Strike up the Band

ALMOST EVERY TOWN in Contra Costa had its own cornet band in the 1880s. Concord had its Silver Band, Martinez its military band. Pittsburg, Pinole, Antioch, Richmond, and Bay Point simply went by the names of their respective hometowns painted on the bands' big bass drums.

The Martinez Military Band was organized in 1887, and raised enough money to buy uniforms and shiny domed helmets by the spring of 1888.

But before the new uniforms arrived in April, the Native Sons of the Golden West, Mt. Diablo Parlor No. 101, requested an appearance of the band at the train depot at the end of Ferry Street.

It seemed that a delegation of Native Sons would be passing through Martinez on its way to a meeting of the Grand Parlor in Fresno, and the local parlor wanted to put on a little welcoming show. The train was to arrive at the Martinez station at 9 p.m.

A small boy carried a sign reading "Mt. Diablo, No. 101, N.S.G.W.," and stood in front of the band.

"As the train pulled into the station the band struck up a lively air, and the crowd of ladies and gentlemen stretched their necks to catch a glimpse of the Native Sons, but in vain, for no one appeared on the platform or the coaches to acknowledge the courtesies extended. Just as the train started out, someone on board shouted in a voice that was distinctly heard above the music of the band, 'Three cheers for the Salvation Army,' and as the last car passed the crowd, and the band ceased playing, a shout of laughter went up from the crowd at the idea of the Martinez Band being taken for the Salvation Army. The joke was greatly enjoyed."

Band shows off new uniforms

The first time the band was able to show off its new uniforms was at the Oddfellows picnic on April 26, a Thursday. It was sponsored by the Martinez and Pacheco Lodges at Cox's Grove, celebrating the lodge's 69th anniversary.

According to the *Gazette:*

"The day was bright and pleasant, and the gentle balmy air of spring, scented with perfume, added greatly to the charm. The grounds were nice and clean and the rustic seats beneath the shade of the overhanging foliage furnished ample room for groups of picnickers to sit and chat and rest after their long ride.

"The Martinez Military Band furnished music for the occasion and attired in their handsome uniforms added materially to the attractiveness of the celebration. The Band left Martinez shortly before eight o'clock in Bennett's coach and arrived at the grounds at 11 o'clock.

"A serenade was tendered each town through which they passed and hearty cheers were returned by the inhabitants."

The *Gazette* reported that "hundreds of teams were tied to the trees, and buggies without number were stationed at all sides of the picnic grounds."

The ladies of the San Ramon Methodist Church were very happy with the event. They sold ice cream, soda water, lemonade, and baked goods, and made a $100 for the church.

Excursion to Tiburon

In the middle of May the Martinez Military Band went down to the wharf to serenade a picnic excursion to Laurel Grove at Point Tiburon. The event was sponsored by the Catholic organization, Young Men's Institutes of Vallejo, Benicia, and Martinez. Tickets for the round trip were $4 for adults and 50 cents for children.

"The steamer left the wharf at Martinez about 7 o'clock and amid the merry shouts of the excursionists and the music of the Martinez Military Band, steered for Benicia."

By the time the steamer picked up its passengers in Martinez, Port Costa, Crockett, and Vallejo there were 1,180 picnickers on board. The revelers didn't reach their destination until 2 p.m. Then they spent three hours at the picnic grounds and boarded the steamer again for home. The steamer didn't dock at the Martinez wharf until 11 p.m. that night. The Y.M.I. picnic was a

Every business decorated for the big Fourth of July celebration in Martinez.
Flags hung on the Reception Saloon, and a horse sported a beer ad.

bigger financial success than the one sponsored by the I.O.O.F.
The Y.M.I. members made $300 profit.

At the end of May the Martinez Military Band elected George
McMahon president, accepted John L. Chase as a new member,
and probably discussed what would be the biggest event of that
year, Martinez's Fourth of July celebration.

The town started planning the celebration early that spring.
By the beginning of May the Fourth of July Committee, headed
by long-time County Clerk L. C. Wittenmyer, had raised $700 to
finance the affair.

Big Fourth of July celebration

Gen. G. W. Bowie was invited to be president of the day, and
Charles Sumner, the orator. Mrs. W. F. Lynch of Walnut Creek was
asked to read the Declaration of Independence. In addition there
would be foot races, tugs of war, and a seven-inning baseball
game. In the evening there would be fireworks and the grand
ball, with music supplied by the Martinez Military Band.

Fourth of July 1888 turned out to be a warm day in Martinez with a slight breeze blowing off the Carquinez Strait.

"At an early hour the vehicles began to arrive from other parts of the county, many from long distances, crowds of happy people in holiday attire, presenting a gay and attractive sight. The trains from the city also brought a large contingent.

"The procession was formed at the depot and the march commenced shortly before 11 a.m. led by the Marshal and aides on horseback, followed by the Martinez Military Band."

Thirty-eight little girls, representing the 38 states, rode on the Goddess of Liberty float. Hermine Blum took the role of the goddess.

Funeral directors Curry & Jones paraded their team of horses, and the Concord Hose and Ladder Company marched with its fire truck. Among the commercial displays was the boat of the Italian fishermen riding a truck covered with a canvass painted with sea views. Even the Pacheco vegetable wagon and the Hofburg Beer wagon were included in the parade.

Only a few arrests for drunkenness

All along the parade route the houses and business were decorated with flags and red, white, and blue bunting.

On July 7, 1888 the *Gazette* reported:

"Everything passed off smoothly and pleasantly on Independence Day. Save one or two drunken and disorderly men, the peace was remarkably well kept.

"An Italian named Tiffi was badly frightened by a firecracker exploding in his face. Horatio Slater was badly burned about the eyes with a redhead firecracker. A Chinese laundryman, with whom the boys were having considerable sport by exploding a firecracker and chaser under his door on Tuesday evening, is said to have fired a pistol shot into the crowd without effect. . . . It is rumored that considerable money changed hands between individuals on the result of the various races on the Fourth. . . . The ball given by the Martinez Military Band was a success both socially and financially."

The dance lasted until 3:30 a.m., and the Military Band netted an $80 profit.

The Day the Banks Closed

WHEN DAWN BROKE in the San Ramon valley on Thursday, March 2, 1933, people got up to what seemed to be another ordinary day.

The *Courier-Journal* had gone to press as usual.

San Ramon High athletes, who beat their counterparts at Livermore the previous week, were preparing for an inter-class track meet.

Mrs. H. J. Hansen was advertising her furnished three-room bungalow, with a breakfast nook, bathroom, and garage at 1627 Oakland Blvd. in Walnut Creek for $20 a month. Annie Van Gorden was planning to finish the birthday cake her friends from the Walnut Creek American Legion Auxiliary brought her Wednesday to celebrate her 80th birthday.

The Safeway Store had posted its five-day sale offering White Star tuna for 12 cents a six-ounce can.

"The Conquerors," featuring Richard Dix and Ann Harding,

The Bank of America on Main Street in Walnut Creek closed its doors when Gov. James Rolph declared a bank holiday on March 2, 1933.

was starting its two-day run at the State Theater in Martinez, where the general admission was 30 cents, loges 40 cents, balcony 20 cents, and children 10 cents.

However, it wasn't to be an ordinary day. When customers arrived at the Bank of America in Walnut Creek that Thursday morning they found they couldn't withdraw or deposit any money.

Gov. James Rolph, Republican, late that Wednesday met with Jared Sullivan, president of the California Bankers Association, Edward Elliot, vice-president of the Security First National Bank of Los Angeles, and W. R. Williams, vice president of the Bank of America. Depositors had been making a record number of withdrawals. When the meeting was over, Rolph declared a three-day bank holiday.

Record withdrawals force closures

The Bank of America, seeking to calm its depositors, published advertisements in local papers featuring the cable of the Golden Gate Bridge, which was then under construction.

"United like the strands of a mighty cable . . . 410 branches united in strength, spirit and service. Each branch has the strength of all."

Whether the ad helped John Mitchell, manager of the Walnut Creek Bank of America branch, explain what was going on to his customers is not known. What is known is that Mitchell spent most of Thursday trying to convince people he had nothing to do with the bank's closing. It was the governor, he said.

Rolph defended his action by telling Californians, "A financial unrest exists throughout the United States, the adverse affect of which has been reflected in the state of California with a consequent unnecessary withdrawal from financial institutions in this state."

Indeed, the Great Depression had been felt in the state. Farm income in 1932 was half of what it had been in 1929, and the number of building permits issued in the Golden State was less than one-ninth of what it was in 1929. Unemployment was climbing. Within another year 1,250,000 Californians, or one-fifth of the state's population, would be on relief.

$2 a day and no work

In Walnut Creek the local relief association tried to find jobs for 13 men with families. Otis Linn, chairman of the Red Cross, reported that the men had been promised three days of work a week at $2 a day in local gardens. But the promise fell through. The people who had signed up to provide the jobs said the weather was too wet or too cold to work or they weren't quite ready. In short, there was no work.

Linn said that one man with a family of seven worked four days in February.

"It takes very little imagination to realize that the children have been suffering through the lack of proper food, proper warmth and sufficient clothing," editorialized the *Courier-Journal.*

Rolph was wrong about the bank holiday lasting three days. On March 4 Franklin Delano Roosevelt became the 32nd president of the United States, and two days later he closed all the banks in the country to stop the massive "runs" that threatened to destroy the banking system of the United States.

On March 9, 1933 the *Walnut Kernal* reported:

"The bank holiday continues today with business in southern Contra Costa County going on as usual. When the banks closed suddenly last Thursday many businessmen were in a quandary as to what to do. Some of them announced they would continue to accept checks from regular customers, but would not cash any checks.

"Others, which had been doing a cash business, agreed to extend temporary credit. Others refused everything but cash. Trade continued as usual, Saturday being a fair day even in those stores which would receive only cash.

"Some merchants put in their safety deposit boxes or home safes the cash they took in, creating a shortage of coin."

Doing business without banks

While there was no real business going on at the Walnut Creek branch of the Bank of America, the manager, John Mitchell, kept the doors open to make change and to allow people to get to their safety deposit boxes.

In the meantime rumors continue to circulate that banks

would remained closed indefinitely and that the bankers if pressed for money would open the safety deposit boxes and remove any and all cash.

Mitchell again was busy denying the rumors. He told anyone who would listen that only the federal government and tax collectors can take money out of safety deposit boxes.

Local chain store managers took their receipts into their Oakland headquarters when they found that they couldn't deposit them in Walnut Creek. The receipts were then used to pay wages and buy more merchandize.

The E-Z-Way-Groceteria stores in both Walnut Creek and Danville announced in their Thursday ads that they were taking customers' checks for groceries.

Maude Silver, associate editor of the *Courier-Journal*, reported that business actually picked up during the second week of the bank holiday. She said it may be that the new president had restored the people's confidence.

"The moratorium is bringing out the cash that has been hidden in the old-sock by those who have been awaiting such eventualities. Despite the fact that very few of the food stores in Walnut Creek have been accepting checks instead of a retardation of business, it has been the reverse, an impetus has been given to business, which up to the moratorium had been somewhat sluggish."

On March 16 the bank holiday was over. The state legislature passed three emergency measures, including a 60-day moratorium on all mortgage foreclosures on dwellings and farms, an emergency bank bill patterned after the federal bank act permitting the reopening of state banks under close supervision, and an emergency building and loan bill restricting withdrawals to $25 or 1 percent, and setting the maximum rate of interest on deposits at 5 percent and the maximum interest on loans at 7.1 percent.

Some banks didn't reopen. But the Bank of America did. Manager John Mitchell reported that deposits were heavier than usual and that no one asked for cash excepting in small quantities to meet ordinary living and business needs.

The Bank of America ran another ad thanking the people of California for their "patience and tolerance."

Murder in the Redwoods

WHEN JAMES WALLACE filed for 147 acres of public land south of the Moraga Grant, he didn't realize the action would culminate in his brother's murder one moonlit night in September 1888.

All Wallace wanted was a place to get away from his coffee and tea business in the turmoil and dust of the bustling, growing town of Oakland in the 1880s.

After James Wallace had filed his claim, he discovered it was landlocked. In order to gain access he needed a 300-foot portion of the Moraga Grant in Redwood Canyon.

Redwood Canyon, then as now, was a lovely, wooded retreat, eight miles from downtown Oakland. It was a place where one could relax for weekend or a couple of weeks. There was a stream that ran through it.

The Redwood Canyon area had once been the biggest and the busiest community on the east side of San Francisco Bay. A redwood forest covered both sides of the hills separating what are now Alameda and Contra Costa counties. That forest provided the redwood to build San Francisco during the Gold Rush. When voters ratified the California constitution, in 1849, the polling place in the redwoods had more voters than either Martinez or San Antonio (which later became part of Oakland.)

The loggers had made short work of the redwoods. By the late 1850s most of the tall trees were gone and only the stumps remained. And by 1885, when the Wallace brothers discovered Redwood Canyon, the canyon's steep slopes were covered with second growth timber. However, the logging industry was history.

The hill and canyon land, which Wallace wanted, wasn't good for wheat or barley. It was grazing land. A few farmers planted orchards. But some enterprising folks regarded the area as a recreation area for Oakland residents. The Wallaces could be counted among those.

Saloon-keeper Harry Bird

Redwood Canyon had few permanent residents. Harry Bird was one. Apparently he had already established an outdoor camping retreat. The place had a rather notorious reputation, and was called "Saints Rest" by the locals. Bird also operated a restaurant-saloon with an attached hotel. He kept a cow, hogs, and a few chickens. He owned several dogs. His nearest neighbors were Andrew Hansen and his wife. They kept a cow and a few chickens. There was bad blood between the Hansens and Bird. Both claimed the same piece of land.

Once when Hansen's wife attempted to retrieve her cow from Bird's pasture, Bird picked Mrs. Hansen up and threw her over the fence. In spite of Bird's temper, he turned out to be helpful when the Wallaces first came to Redwood Canyon.

The Moraga Land Grant, of which Redwood Canyon formed a portion, was controlled by the cunning Oakland attorney Horace Carpentier. He was a well-known land grabber who had successfully helped himself to Spanish land grant after Spanish land grant. In order to buy the portion he needed, Wallace dealt with Carpentier's agent, John Watson. It was Bird who took Wallace to Watson's farm, six miles from Moraga.

According to Wallace, Watson assured him there would be no problem in getting the access. He advised him to improve the 300-foot strip of land he needed by building a house, fences, and planting an orchard. Wallace did what Watson told him, spending more than $2,500. In all, Wallace fenced in between 10 and 12 acres on both sides of the stream. He planted a few apple trees and built two bridges.

A retreat in the redwoods

From 1885 through 1888 both James and George Wallace came out to stay at what they called the "Wallace Camp." James brought his family to stay a week at a time. There were also other guests, who paid for the privilege of putting up tents on the Wallace property. It was rumored that Bird wasn't happy about the competition for his own business. However, when Wallace paid $3.60 in personal property taxes in 1886 on the improvements of the Redwood Canyon property, Bird apparently handled the matter with the tax collector. The next year taxes went up to $5.20, because by then Wallace had added a cow, a calf, chickens, and a wagon to his personal property in Contra Costa. Again Bird served as the agent. And the land itself was still owned by Carpentier. Every time Wallace wanted to pay for the land or at least get something in writing, Watson told him there was no hurry.

Watson, unfortunately, died before anything was ever written down. When Wallace tried to buy the land from the new agent, he was told he couldn't. Carpentier was going to sell all 13,000 acres of the grant to one buyer. Wallace could lease the land for $100 a year, payable immediately.

Wallace wouldn't pay and was served notice on March 28, 1888 to vacate in three days. George Wallace was living on the property at the time and refused to leave. Bird, probably working with the Carpentier interests, tore down the Wallace fence, which George Wallace put back. By the time the issue got to court, the two men disliked each other intensely.

In May 1888 James Wallace told his story in Contra Costa Superior Court in Martinez. He admitted he had no written contract with the late John Watson. Wallace produced a witness, Frank Leighton.

Leighton testified that Watson had told him Wallace had his permission to build a little camp for a place of recreation, and eventually would buy the piece of land. In addition, Leighton said that Watson was regarded by everyone in Redwood Canyon and Moraga as Carpentier's agent.

Leighton's testimony wasn't good enough for the jury, which decided in favor of the Carpentier interests. Wallace appealed. On September 25, 1888 the court denied the appeal. On September 26 George Wallace was dead and Harry Bird was in jail.

"A cold blooded murder took place at the roadside hotel in Redwood Canyon Tuesday evening in which George Wallace is the victim. Henry Bird the proprietor of the hotel is charged with the crime," reported the *Contra Costa Gazette* on September 29, 1888.

For the next four months Harry Bird remained locked up in County Jail while his attorneys went through a variety of legal maneuvers. Finally, on January 10, 1889, Bird's trial began. It took four days. On January 14 the jury found him guilty of murder in the first degree. And by January 29th Bird was on his way to San Quentin to begin serving a life sentence.

John Nielson, a sailor from Denmark, was one of the first witnesses called by the prosecution. He was out of work when he met James Wallace, proprietor of the New York Tea Co., in Oakland. Wallace owned a camping ground in Redwood Canyon, which was operated by his brother, George.

"I was speaking about going into the country to take a little rest, and Mr. Wallace said, if you would like to go up to the camp you can go up there and stay there, so I went up there," Nielson explained to the jury.

Nielson walked the eight miles from Oakland to Redwood Canyon, carrying his clothes in a small black valise. He arrived on Friday, September 21, 1888. George Wallace, James's brother, welcomed him, and the two lived in the three-room house that was the main building on the campsite.

When Eli Chase, the defense attorney, asked what the two did during the four days preceding the murder, Nielson said, "Well, we didn't do nothing, only hanging on."

On Tuesday evening the two finished supper at 8 p.m., and George asked if Nielson would like to go see a countryman of his. Andrew Hansen and his wife lived a half-mile into the canyon from the Wallace Camp. Harry Bird's saloon and hotel, called Saint's Rest, was between the Wallace house and the Hansens.

Nielson testified that lights were on at the saloon when they passed. Dogs were barking. Wallace said something about the dogs, but defense attorney Chase quickly objected to Nielson's repeating Wallace's words, and was sustained by Judge Joseph Jackson. Nielson and Wallace stayed at the Hansens, talking until midnight. They did not drink any alcohol. In fact, Nielson said that in the four days he had been at the camp, he never saw Wallace take a drink.

Murderer jumps off porch

By the time the two started walking back to the Wallace camp, the moon had risen. It was midnight. As they passed the saloon arm in arm, a man rose from the bench on the porch.

"Saints Rest" in Redwood Canyon.

"(He) just jumped up and swung some kind of an instrument there and knocked Mr. Wallace over the head with it and Mr. Wallace made a groan. I let go his arm and he staggered forward."

Nielson pulled a gun out of his pocket, and as he fired he saw a flash of a shot coming towards him and Wallace.

"I fired after that flash and in return I got a shot fired after me; then I thought it was for me and I turned and went up to Mr. Hansen's."

Nielson identified the attacker as the defendant, Harry Bird.

The shots were heard by several men in the saloon. All, including Bird, had been drinking heavily since 7 p.m. They testified that Bird had come into the bar room and told them there was a drunk on the road and he wanted him arrested. Bird got one of the patrons to wake up deputy constable Ed Rankin, who happened to be staying at Bird's hotel. Rankin put Bird under arrest after he found Wallace's dead body and a gun in Bird's pocket.

The most damaging testimony against Bird came from Deputy Sheriff C. W. Rogers, who talked to Bird at the County Jail, after the murder.

"He (Bird) said, 'God knows, I ought not to be here alone . . .

there is others that ought to be in with me. . . . My God, I waited for that fellow, when he come along, I knocked him, but I did not do the shooting.'"

As a result of Bird's statement, two saloon patrons were arrested, but charges were dropped against both of them after the preliminary hearing. And the two testified for the prosecution in January.

Mystery motive

Andrew Hansen, who claimed the land where Bird had built his saloon, also testified for the prosecution. He said that three hours before the murder Bird had come off his porch in the dark to look at him (Hansen) on his horse. Bird never said a word, and Hansen spurred his horse to get out of Bird's way.

James Smallwood, an Oaklander, who had stayed at the Wallaces' retreat the previous July, was the only witness who testified about any ill-feeling Bird had for George Wallace. Bird told Smallwood that he would like to "gut that bugger"—meaning Wallace.

The trial transcript didn't reveal why Bird hated Wallace enough to kill him. Bird never testified in his own behalf. The only hints at a motive appeared in the *Oakland Tribune*, which reported that Bird repeatedly tore down the Wallaces' fences. The local gossips said that Bird was jealous of the Wallace Camp, believing it was stealing his business. Also there were rumors that Bird actually worked for Oakland attorney Horace Carpentier.

Carpentier took the Wallaces to court to evict them from their camp, which was on his land. He beat the Wallaces in court the day before the murder occurred, and they were facing eviction.

After the trial, Bird paid his attorney, Eli Chase, by deeding over his property in Redwood Canyon. Bird's neighbor, Hansen, already claimed Bird's property. He took over the saloon and operated it. The legal squabbles about the ownership continued until 1903, when Hansen's divorced wife, Mary, and W. M. Watson, who held one of Andrew Hansen's mortgages, were declared co-owners. Chase apparently never earned a dime for defending Bird.

Lin Oy is Missing

PON LIN had gained the respect of the people in Martinez. By 1891 he had been operating a laundry there for quite some time.

The editor of the *Contra Costa Gazette* had seen fit to praise Pon Lin in print.

"If the rest (Chinese immigrants) were all as reliable and upright as Pon Lin there would not be half the prejudice that now exists against the race."

It was no wonder that Pon Lin was given the responsibility in January 1892 to care for one Lin Oy, a Chinese maiden of about 15 years, who had become the ward of the court in Contra Costa County.

The Chinese had arrived in California with the onset of the Gold Rush and had been in Martinez almost from the beginning of that immigration.

Many of the leading families of Contra Costa and Alameda counties had Chinese cooks. John and Louie Strenzel Muir not only hired Chinese cooks, but house cleaners and farm laborers. The Hook family in Pleasant Hill also had a Chinese cook.

The fruit cannery in Martinez employed Chinese cannery workers. And Chinese laborers had laid the tracks of the rail line that came through the town, and had built the levees in the Delta.

But in spite of the Chinese being in Martinez for close to a quarter of a century, a Chinese couple caused quite a stir on November 7, 1891 when Justice of the Peace J. P. Smith performed a marriage ceremony for them.

Lin Oy is a blushing bride

"You Tai, a native of the Flowery Kingdom, and Lin Oy, a blushing damsel of the likewise oriental nativity, have so far broken away from their traditional teachings as to seek a matrimonial alliance after the approved American form. . . . This is the second instance in which a Chinese marriage has been solem-

Carrying the burdens of the daily round.

nized here in accordance with American law and custom," the *Contra Costa Gazette* reported.

There were so few weddings among the Chinese immigrant population in California because there were so few women. The male-to-female ratio in 1890 was 27 to 1. The Chinese did not bring their wives and families when they came to the United States. Most immigrants believed that they would return back home when they accumulated enough savings.

For the most part the few Chinese women who did come to the United States were not wives, but young girls who had been sold or stolen in China and then shipped by dealers to port cities on the Pacific Coast. Once in the United States, these unfortunate women became the property of the Tong masters and were relegated to a life of prostitution. It was reported that these women were used by dozens of men in a single night for less than 50 cents apiece.

Some girls were little more than babies when they were sold in China. They would be sent to the United States, where they would work in the homes of the rich merchants and were raised by the merchants' wives or concubines. This system of bondage didn't bother the American authorities even though the Civil War had put an end to slavery in 1863. The only ones who cared about the plight of the Chinese women seemed to be the Christian missionaries.

Lin Oy was one of these young Chinese women who had come to the United States in 1883.

Bridegroom is jailed

On the marriage license, You Tai swore that he was 33 and his bride, Lin Oy, was 18 and they were both residents of San Francisco. Apparently the couple did not go back to San Francisco after the wedding, for on December 5 the *Gazette* reported that You Tai had been accused of perjury and put in the county jail

At the preliminary hearing before Justice of the Peace Smith, the Rev. J. F. McMasters, pastor of the Chinese Mission in San Francisco, testified that Lin Oy was only 15. She had come to California when she was 5 years old and had been working for one Leong Lam, the inspector and secretary of the Sam Yup Association.

"The damsel was given or sold to Leong Lam, nine years ago, as was stated by Leong Lam himself, who was present and testified in the case. She had been employed as a domestic in his family until quite recently when she ran away, and for a time all trace of her was lost. A reward was offered and eventually her whereabouts was discovered, and she was taken to the Chinese Mission for greater security," according to the *Gazette.*

It might seem curious that Leong Lam would offer a reward for Lin Oy, but she was considered property. He could get from $300 to $2,000 by selling her on the slave market.

Apparently Lin Oy didn't like living and working at the Mission any better than she had liked staying with the Leong Lam family. She escaped from that institution and eloped with You Tai.

Lin Oy is kidnapped

After hearing the testimony, Justice Smith bound You Tai over for trial in Superior Court and set his bail at $2,000. You Tai couldn't come up with the money, and so remained in jail. His bride was sent to live with the laundryman and his wife until the case was to be decided.

On January 2, 1892 two men pounded on the door of Pon Lin's home. It was almost midnight. The laundrymen answered the door and was pushed aside. The two men drew pistols and threatened all inside with death if anyone made a sound.

"One Chinaman endeavored to escape by another door, when he was confronted by four more of the gang, all armed, who quickly stopped his progress. In the meantime the two highbinders who had entered went to the room of the unsuspecting Lin Oy and forcibly took possession of her person and made good their retreat," reported the *Gazette* in its January 6 issue.

Pon Lin did not report the kidnapping of Lin Oy for almost 30 minutes. He was much too frightened. Sheriff Rogers immediately launched a search. Rogers suspected that the gang came by boat and left the same way. He was wrong.

"The whole proceeding was one of astonishing boldness, as the risk was so great of some person seeing them on the street, when their number and strange appearance would have been sure to attract attention. . . . It was determined that the abductors came in buggies obtained at some livery stable and went to Oakland after the raid. Constable Reese Jones is on their track, and there is a good chance of capturing them."

Pon Lin told the sheriff that he suspected Lin Oy's former owner, Leong Lam, to be in back of the kidnapping.

Lin Oy spirited to San Leandro

Three days later the *Gazette* reported that a Mr. Waterbury of Oakland had come forward and disclosed that it was his team of horses and buggy that had been hired to go to Martinez.

"By the aid of the stable keeper, Sheriff Rogers was enabled to hunt up and identify the parties who had hired the rig, and as a result one Toy Juck Ting, a Chinese merchant on Dupont Street (San Francisco) was arrested."

Two others were also identified by the stable keeper and were arrested. They denied they had anything to do with the kidnapping and insisted they had never been to Martinez and didn't even know where it was.

"But on arrival here one of them was instantly recognized as having been a cook in several families and he soon showed himself perfectly familiar with the place and the people. They were admitted to bail in the sum of $500."

The three paid their bail and left town. No trace was found of Lin Oy. The authorities suspected she had been "spirited away to San Leandro. . . . In whose interest she was stolen is not clear but the general opinion is that her alleged owner is at the bottom of the affair."

Two weeks later the suspected kidnappers appeared in court. Charges were dismissed because of lack of evidence. The *Gazette* never reported what became of Lin Oy or even her bridegroom, You Tai. However, Pon Lin made the news on January 30, 1892.

"Chinese New Year was celebrated on Thursday and on Friday morning the sidewalk in front of Pon Lin's laundry works looked as if a cracker factory had blown up."

Byron Train Wreck

RAILROAD TRAVEL was cheap, convenient, and the most practical way to get around California in 1902. Close to 6,000 miles of track crisscrossed the state. For a few dollars, travelers could get to almost every corner of California, but it wasn't always safe.

While the railroad moguls were taking in money by the millions in California, they were reluctant to spend money for safety equipment. In the years 1895–1896, 132 passengers and employees were killed while another 367 were injured in this state alone. However appalling those figures were, it took more lives and more crashes before laws were passed mandating the railroad men to take action.

In 1902 one of those crashes, which finally moved the state to take action, occurred near Byron. Byron was a creature of the railroad, which even gave the little farming community its name. The Central Pacific railroad tracks reached Byron in the far eastern section of Contra Costa County in 1878. It was probably the railroad that prompted Fish & Blum, the big grain merchants of Martinez, to erect a warehouse there in the middle of fertile wheat country, and German-born Henry Wilkening to build his hotel, saloon, and livery stable. Wilkening liked Byron so much that he even named his son after the town.

The railroad also assured the business of a hot springs resort some two and a half miles distant from the town. Orange Risdon Jr. had bought the springs as a possible commercial source for salt. He received a patent in 1865, signed by President Andrew Johnson, and actually built a salt evaporation plant at the springs. It wasn't a success, so Risdon abandoned his salt-making venture and took advantage of the stories about the healing qualities of the springs. Risdon's nephew, Lewis Risdon Meade, joined his uncle, and the two of them started a resort and built a 10-room house to take care of patrons. But travel to the resort was an arduous ride by horse and buggy or wagon until the railroad came to town.

Meade built a wooden hotel, spending the astronomical figure of $50,000. When the hotel burned down, in 1901, Meade rebuilt, spending $150,000 for a three-story, frame-stucco building with a beautiful view of the San Joaquin Valley.

The hot springs resort had made Byron a household name throughout the Bay Area. So on December 20, 1902, when word came about one of the most disastrous train wrecks in California history, everyone reading the newspaper headlines knew where it had happened.

The Owl, which was bound for Los Angeles, was one of the Southern Pacific's most modern trains. It had a diner, drawing room, and sleeping cars. The last car was a day coach added to take care of the extra influx of passengers wanting to get home to the Fresno area for the Christmas holidays.

The train steamed out of the Oakland mole sometime after 4:30 p.m. The train was on time as it pulled into the Oakland 16th Street station and then went north to Richmond, Crockett, Port Costa, and Martinez. At the Cornwall station (Antioch) it headed into the San Joaquin Valley, and shortly after passing Brentwood something happened to what up to then was a speedy, pleasant ride.

"The engine became disabled through a leaky flue. Steam escaped from the flue and put out the fire in the fire box, and the train was brought promptly to a standstill. There happened to be a freight train at Byron and arrangements were being made to have the freight engine haul the Owl into Byron."

The Stockton Flyer, a commuter train, was a half hour behind the Owl. It was delayed at Port Costa, and so engineer James McGuire was speeding down the tracks in order to make up time.

"Byron, December 20.—One of the most serious railroad disasters that has occurred in California in years happened a mile west of here shortly after 7 o'clock this evening when the Stockton flyer crashed into the rear end of the south-bound Owl train, killing and injuring 40 people.

"At midnight ten bodies had been removed from the wreckage and several more were seen pinioned under the weight of debris from which they could not easily be extricated. . . . Of the

Hell of a way to run a railroad.

killed it was possible to identify only one person," reported the *San Francisco Chronicle*.

The rear coach had been crushed into splinters by the impact. All 30 people in the car at the moment of the crash were either killed or injured.

"Dr. Bird of Byron hurried to the scene of the wreck as soon as word of the disaster reached here, and took with him all of the nurses that could be pressed into the service. With Dr. Davidson of Fresno, who was a passenger on the train, he took charge of the work of caring for the injured as they were removed from the wreckage, and later they were assisted by Dr. Theodore Olmsted and Dr. J. T. H. Dunn of Oakland, who arrived on a special train."

Meade, the proprietor of the resort, also came to help bringing more doctors from the resort. Byron residents built fires along the track to warm the victims. Eight of the injured were taken to the Byron Hotel.

Townspeople "risked being scalded to death in helping to recover victims from the wreckage." Deputy Sheriff Le Grande of Byron was joined by Sheriff R. R. Veale, who had been on the

Stockton Flyer that night. Veale and Le Grande pressed railroad hands into patrol service to prevent wholesale looting.

The next day Le Grand told reporters, "I noticed one man searching a pair of trousers and I promptly ran him off the embankment. . . . That many thefts were committed in and about the wreck I have no doubt. Valises were scattered about, and I had some difficulty in getting this and other property together and keeping it safely guarded," said Le Grand. Even the good Dr. Bird was not immune from the thefts. While he was working with the injured, someone walked off with his overcoat.

Within a few days of the Byron train disaster Southern Pacific railroad officials had found a scapegoat for the wreck. They put the blame squarely on the shoulders of the engineer of the Stockton Flyer. Engineer J. M. McGuire had plenty of time to stop his train before it crashed into the rear of the Owl, which had stalled before reaching the Byron station, the manager of the Southern Pacific railroad stated to the *San Francisco Chronicle* on December 22, 1902, two days after the wreck.

"He is solely responsible for the wreck, and I can only attribute the affair to an error on his part in understanding the distance that lay between his train and the rear car of the Owl at the time he saw and answered the signal of the Owl's flagman."

Manager James Agler said the weather was clear and that the track between Brentwood and Byron "is a perfect stretch of straight, level road. Any engineer will tell you that on leaving Brentwood he can see the lights of Byron, over five miles away."

At the time Agler made his statement, no Southern Pacific official had spoken to the hospitalized McGuire. Agler said "We are not so inhuman as to inflict him with the ordeal of questioning him in his present condition." Agler added that "in spite of the statement of the Byron citizen who thought he saw the flagman signaling the approaching train from a position of a few hundred feet behind the Owl, I am satisfied that Brakeman (George) Cole of the Owl went back a sufficient distance to flag the approaching Stockton train . . . not less than 1,600 feet."

Filling up the Martinez morgue

Of the 27 people who died as a result of that train wreck, 12 were taken to a makeshift morgue in Martinez. It was Contra Costa County's biggest train disaster to date. Coroner Henry J. Curry, who was also Martinez' mortician, never had handled so many bodies at one time.

The Martinez inquest wasn't the only one that resulted from the wreck. All the counties to which victims were taken and where they later died also held inquests, which included San Francisco, Alameda, and Fresno.

Curry had been in the undertaking business for 11 years when the Byron wreck occurred. He got into the business through his livery stable. People at the time thought this was quite logical, since the livery stable owner was often called upon to deliver bodies to cemeteries. Curry not only was the town's mortician but later organized the Sunset View Cemetery Association.

It was the testimony of Byron farmers at the Martinez inquest that contradicted Southern Pacific officials.

"When the Owl passed . . . Saturday evening it was going so slow he (Charles Copel) was at first inclined to think it was a freight, but on closer inspection learned it was the Owl. W. M. Moore, a farmer residing near Byron, testified that on the night of the wreck he was standing about 500 feet away from the track and was quite positive that when the signal was given by the flagman and answered by McGuire the Flyer was within 200 feet of the rear end of the Owl," reported the *Chronicle*.

No time to stop the train

When McGuire finally did speak, he testified that he saw the lights of the Owl sometime after he left Brentwood, but thought it was sitting on a siding at the Byron station. He didn't see the flagman until he was within 200 feet of the train. Other testimony revealed that the Flyer was going 55 miles an hour between Brentwood and Byron. It was speeding in order to make up for lost time when it had stopped at Port Costa.

McGuire told the coroners' juries that instead of the 1,600 feet that Southern Pacific officials said was needed to stop the train, he needed 3,500 feet because the track between Brentwood and Byron was not level—it had a slight downhill grade.

With coroners' juries meeting from Fresno to San Francisco,

the Bay Area papers carried stories of other railroad wrecks during the same period.

On December 22, a freight train jumped the track and fell over a precipice near Emigrant Gap. No one was reported injured. On December 23 the Sacramento local passenger train collided with a special freight at Thirteenth avenue in Oakland. The engineer and conductor of the freight train were blamed and were fired immediately by the Southern Pacific manager, Agler. The only injury seemed to be to the engineer of the Sacramento train. On December 24, the papers reported that a Santa Fe freight was wrecked near Bakersfield. Also, on Christmas Eve that year, 10 people were killed in Colorado in a wreck between a freight train and a coal train. On December 28, 28 people were killed in a head-on collision between a freight train and a passenger express on the Grand Trunk line in Ontario, Canada.

While the railroads tended to put the blame on human error, newspapers had different ideas.

"The Southern Pacific Company seems to be experiencing another epidemic of train wrecks which periodically afflict it," editorialized the *San Francisco Chronicle*. It accused the Southern Pacific of trying to operate "two-track traffic on a single line," relying on conductors and brakemen for safety purposes instead of hiring regular switchmen. The paper also attacked the railroad for overworking its engineers instead of hiring more people.

"Parsimony is at the bottom of accidents . . . and the responsibility for them must rest with those in authority."

The various official inquiries found that the crews of both the Flyer and the Owl were operating within company rules, but noted that until the railroad instituted a signal system that would maintain space between trains, these types of accidents would be repeated.

In the year ending June 30, 1903 (the year that the Byron disaster occurred), 1,059 people were killed in train wrecks and 10,864 injured.

Squatters Win One

THE GRAIN CROP was growing just fine on April 17, 1883, so naturally John Dolan was upset when he saw Joe Mugnemi trample through it with a load of lumber and eight men armed with rifles and pistols.

But as a result of the action Dolan took, he later found himself before Justice of the Peace Milo Turner in Walnut Creek, charged with malicious mischief.

Dolan was employed by San Francisco lawyer Joseph Naphtaly, who owned nearly 1,500 acres in what later became Rossmoor. Naphtaly started buying land southwest of Walnut Creek in 1869, and his biggest problem for the next 20 years was squatters.

When Dolan appeared before Judge Turner he testified about the second time he saw Mugnemi, which was nine days later.

"I next saw him (on April 26) with another load of lumber guarding it with a gun on the land owned by Naphtaly. 'Who has taken possession of this land?' I ask. He then leveled and pointed a loaded gun at me and ordered me to halt."

Mugnemi built a cabin guarded by armed men, Dolan said. Building the cabin destroyed the growing crop.

After a month, it was obvious to Dolan that Mugnemi was not

VINEYARD & FARM OF JOSEPH NAPHTALY NEAR WALNUT CREEK, CONTRA COSTA, CO.

going to go away peaceably. On May 22, Dolan and three assistants went to the cabin.

"I took a shotgun with me to protect my life. I was afraid 'Italian Joe' (Mugnemi) would shoot me was the reason I took the shotgun. The reason I removed that cabin was this: I am in charge of that land to keep off trespassers. I used no more force than was absolutely necessary."

Under cross-examination, Dolan said:

"I presented my gun and told Italian Joe to throw up his hands. I asked him who was inside and he said, 'Tipple.' I told him to tell him to come out. Tipple came out dressed but in his stocking feet. He then put on his boots.

"I told the men with me to go in and get the firearms. They did so. Then I told them to fire them off, which they did. There was one shotgun and three revolvers.

"I told Italian Joe to go in the cabin and take out his effects. There was a wagon on the ground, and we helped Joe take out his private effects and after taking them out, I ordered the men to tear down the cabin. I then sent a man to get a team and haul away the lumber."

Testifying for the prosecution, Mugnemi said that Dolan showed up at his cabin about 4:30 a.m. May 22. "They ordered me to throw up my hands and pointed a shotgun at me. I threw up my hands and they advanced towards the house and commenced to throw out my provisions."

Mugnemi claimed that the cabin was his house.

"I used it to live in. I was living in it at this time. I built the house with the help of others. The value of the house was $15 to $25."

Under cross-examination, Mugnemi admitted he built the cabin on top of the grain crop and inside a fence.

"I don't know who built the fence," he said.

The judge sided with Mugnemi. He found Dolan guilty, fined him $50 and ordered him to spend 30 days in the County Jail.

Despite occasional setbacks like this one, Naphtaly eventually prevailed over squatters.

By 1897, he was known throughout the area for his 140-acre

vineyard and distillery, where Del Valle High School was later built. Naphtaly also had pear and apple orchards.

In 1930, the Naphtaly family sold the land to R. Stanley Dollar, son of shipping magnate Robert Dollar. Dollar turned the ranch into a showplace and sold it to Rossmoor Corp. 30 years later.

Concord's Own Fire Dancer

THE FIRE DANCER PAPINTA, yards of silk swirling about her body, gets rave reviews from San Francisco to Cape Town at the turn of the century.

"She is the everglittering spectacular, with its roses and lilies, butterflies and birds, that mysteriously rise and form flames of fire in the greatest of all performances, the serpentine dance with its countless yards of titillating silks and long sticks, which are so skillfully handled by this queen of all danseuses."

So wrote the *Richmond Record* in 1901.

None of Papinta's costumes has fewer than 150 yards of material, and the one she uses for her flame dance takes 520 yards. Papinta uses mirrors and calcium arc lamps to create multiple images on stage.

The little girl from Indiana, Caroline Hipple Holpin, seemingly has it all—a zooming dance career, a husband who adores her, and a ranch five miles south of Concord in the Ygnacio Valley.

Her triumph doesn't last long.

Papinta's life starts downhill March 11, 1905.

A telegram arrives from California when she is on stage in Rochester, N.Y. Her husband, William J. Holpin, 35, has died at their ranch of "acute gastritis."

She has been on tour and hasn't seen him since November. During the five-day train ride home to the funeral in Ygnacio Valley, Papinta has time to remember.

They were both 19 when they married in Chicago on the morning of May 10, 1887.

Holpin, who grew up in Wisconsin, was an athlete and a lover of horse racing and the theater. The couple moved often those first years, from Omaha to Denver to Portland. Then to San Francisco, Minneapolis, and back to Chicago.

It was in Chicago that Billy Holpin convinced his wife to do the flame dance. They bought a complicated set of mirrors called the "crystal maze," which reflected lights from calcium arc lamps.

Papinta, the fire dancer, performed on three continents, but her favorite spot on Earth was her ranch in the Ygnacio Valley.

Holpin found Caroline a teacher and had her "trained." Within a few years she played the European capitols, and the two decided to invest her earnings in a West Coast rancho.

In 1897 they bought 100 acres for $8,000 in Ygnacio Valley, where Holpin could fulfill his dream of raising racehorses.

In 1901 the *Richmond Record* called the Papinta Stock Farm a showplace.

"Live oaks dot the place, and, back of the house, a narrow creek flows lazily along its gully. . . . All sorts of sylvan loveliness about, and there are wildflowers, ferns and bits of beauty in abundance. . . . On each side of the road leading to the house a great number of palms have been planted. . . . The whole farm had been piped for water from a private supply source, and all the buildings are illuminated by electricity from a private dynamo."

Papinta has Billy's last letter with her as she makes the trip west.

"I feel exactly we have a future here in this place with my only love 'you.' I am willing to live and die here," he had written.

Once back in Contra Costa, not only does Papinta have to deal with her husband's death, but also with her greedy father-in-law, James Holpin.

He is a drifter, going from job to job. At times he worked for his son and Papinta on the stock farm. Within a few months of his son's death, Holpin sues his daughter-in-law. He contends that Billy and Papinta were never married and that she has no claim on the rancho.

Papinta claims that she and her husband made identical wills, leaving the stock farm to each other. Her husband kept his will in his trunk, but it has disappeared along with their marriage license, she says.

In any case, it was her salary that bought the rancho and the horses, she testifies.

"Was any money ever earned in horse racing?" the attorney asks.

"Never," answers Papinta.

"Was any lost?"

"Yes."

"Who paid for the losses?"

"I did," she says.

Papinta produces two attorneys from Chicago who testify that they drew up the Holpins' wills. She also introduces Billy's last letter.

Her father-in-law's attorney wants Papinta to reveal her age during his questioning.

"And what is your age please?"

"Oh. I don't see how I can say that. I won't say it. You don't want to ruin me. . . . I am not going to tell it."

But she does.

"I am 37 to tell the truth. It is an awful thing to admit, but I hope to retire soon so it won't make much difference."

The judge decides in her favor on September 21, 1906, 1½ years after her husband's death. At the time Papinta has just completed a successful tour of Johannesburg and Cape Town, and plans a tour of Europe for 1907.

Papinta's brother, George Hipple, is her stage manager for the European trip. Her six-week run in Berlin is a success.

She has just finished her evening performance in Dusseldorf on August 10, 1907. She is her usual serene self.

Hipple goes to remove her equipment from the stage. Minutes later, Papinta's maid calls to him that her mistress is desperately ill. He rushes to the dressing room.

Too late. Papinta is dead. It is speculated that the fumes from the arc lamps had something to do with her sudden death.

Papinta is buried next to her beloved Billy and his mother at Alhambra Cemetery, Martinez. She leaves the rancho to her brother George.

The *Concord Transcript* eulogizes her with the headline, "The Curtain Falls on Papinta."

"She contemplated spending happy years on the ranch she loved so well near Concord. It is for us to propose and God to dispose."

Shoot-out in Old Clayton

HE'D KILLED ONE MAN over land rights. Now he was warning another. Clayton neighbors steered clear of "Doc" William Rider Powell that spring of 1904.

The old man had just gotten out of the Martinez jail. He was just as mean when he got out as when he went in. He had a habit of carrying a pistol in a gunnysack.

Powell lived in an old San Francisco horse-drawn streetcar on his property on Marsh Creek Road. He only had two horses. Both were old. He went to jail after he threatened his neighbor, Manual Cardoza.

The argument was over 80 acres Cardoza leased from the railroad for grazing land. Powell, who had dreams of working the quicksilver mine in the area, said he had staked a mining claim to the land and no one else should be on it.

He told Cardoza to give back the lease and get his money back from the railroad company.

Cardoza took Powell seriously and swore out a complaint. Two years earlier the old man had shot and killed Albert Crandall over the same thing.

John Bendixen was a witness to the Crandall killing. Bendixen and Crandall lived in a house on the hill just above Powell's railroad car. They used the quicksilver mine road to get to the main road to Concord. There was a gate on the road, but it hadn't been closed in 15 years.

On February 12, 1902, Powell pulled the gate shut across the road.

"Albert and myself come down in a buggy. We had this wild colt. It was the first time it was hitched onto the buggy. I was driving," testified Bendixen at the preliminary hearing.

Powell was at the gate fixing something. Crandall told Bendixen to "hang onto the colt. I'll go and open the gate."

"Doc, what are you shutting this gate for. We don't want no gate here. Powell, you better get on that old white horse and get away from here. You got no business here," Bendixen reported Crandall's warning.

Crandall waved his arms.

Powell didn't answer. He just walked towards his horse. Crandall followed him. There was a sack on the ground.

"Then he stopped still. Crandall stopped still. The defendant picked up the sack, pulled out a pistol, cocked it and shot him dead," said Bendixen.

"How many times did he shoot?" asked the prosecutor.

"Once."

The crack of the pistol frightened Bendixen's horse. It bolted and ran up the road toward the house.

"He made two or three shots at me. He says, 'I'll get you too, you old. . . .' Then he shot at me," said Bendixen.

Bendixen went back to his own house to get his Winchester rifle, and headed back to see what he could do for Crandall.

"I went to see if he was dead or alive, whether I had to send for a doctor or a coroner. I just went and looked at his face and I see he was dead. I pulled off my old coat and covered him over and took my hat and covered his face," said Bendixen.

Powell admitted he killed Crandall. He claimed that Crandall was coming after him and that he was only defending himself. The jury believed him.

But two years later, when Powell ordered Cardoza off the railroad land and testified before Justice of the Peace Gus Goethals that he would hurt anyone who tried to come onto his land, Goethals didn't take any chances.

When Powell couldn't come up with a $2,500 bond to "insure the peace," Constable Charles Chapman took him to jail.

Powell was released within a month. By that time his hay crop was ready for mowing. He hitched his horse to his ancient buggy and went over the hills to Oakland to find someone to cut it. No one in Clayton wanted to work for him.

Powell hired Joseph Adams, a junk peddler, who apparently wasn't doing so well buying and selling at the Oakland free market. When the two arrived back in Clayton on June 4, 1904, Powell saw Cardoza's small herd of cattle grazing on land he considered his territory.

Albert Crandall, a victim of "Doc" Powell.

He started to chase them off, but then Cardoza appeared with a gun.

"You let that stock alone," Cardoza shouted.

Powell took his gun out of the gunnysack and headed toward the gate to let the cattle out. Cardoza shouted again and again, "Keep away from the gate."

Powell waved his pistol in his right hand and opened the gate with his left. Cardoza raised his gun. A shot rang out. Powell fell over the open gate.

Adams rushed over.

"I'm shot through and through. I think I'm killed," said Powell.

"Well, Doc, I'll go after the doctor," said Adams.

"Hell with the doctor. Doctor couldn't save me. I'm bound to die. I'll be dead before you get back," he said.

Powell didn't die until the next morning, at County Hospital. A jury found that Cardoza had acted in self-defense.

When Powell's daughter went to dispose of his estate, she found that he had mortgaged the mine, which he didn't legally own, to the attorney who had defended him in the Crandall case. She sold the 160 acres her father did own for $12 an acre. The two horses brought $5 apiece.

The Great Tire Contest

BY 1913 THE AUTOMOBILE was just beginning to change the lives of Concord citizens.

Advertisements for automobiles and horse-drawn wagons appeared side by side in the *Concord Transcript*. Johnson's Garage in Martinez was selling Ford touring cars for $675.—"Get in your order now as they are hard to get."

Joseph Boyd, a blacksmith by trade, had the agency for the Studebaker horse-drawn wagon and the Studebaker automobile.

"Studebaker wagons are built of good stuff. They're made right by people who've had years and years of experience in making them right," read Boyd's ad.

Frederick Galindo, owner of the Concord Mercantile Co. general store on Salvio and Mt. Diablo streets, was one of the town merchants who switched in 1913 from the horse-drawn delivery wagon to a motorized vehicle.

With the purchase of the Studebaker Auto Delivery vehicle, Galindo promised to deliver goods not only in Concord but throughout the surrounding county.

In April 1913 the Concord city fathers decided that what the growing town really needed was a speed limit.

Henry Botts, a town trustee and another town blacksmith, made the motion that speed limit signs be erected on all roads leading into town, and that the marshal be instructed to arrest "each and every person" violating the limit. Town Trustee Galindo seconded the motion.

The editor of the *Concord Transcript*, S. W. Holcomb, had been pushing for a 10-mph limit, but trustees decided that a 15-mph limit would be better. Besides setting a speed limit, the new law also decreed that drivers would have to signal when turning their vehicles from the curb into the street.

"The driver shall give a signal that can be plainly seen from the rear of such vehicle. . . . The signal can be made by raising the hand or a whip."

Anyone caught exceeding the speed limit would have to pay a $300 fine or go to County Jail. Each day in jail would count as $2 toward the fine.

Galindo's daughter, Ruth—a retired schoolteacher, Concord historian, and descendent of early Spanish settlers—remembers that her father loved cars.

"I remember driving wherever we went. He taught me to drive when I was 14. I don't know how many blowouts we had one time when we went driving through Franklin Canyon."

While customers could get everything from shovels to groceries and $2 corsets at Galindo's store in April 1913, they couldn't buy tires.

Then traveling salesman E. L. Hiteman came to town the last week of April.

The story of how Galindo came to carry the Diamond Silvertown Cord Tire was revealed on the front pages of the *Concord Transcript*.

Just before the Automobile Age, when the local blacksmith could fix anything that was worth fixing.

"Mr. F. C. Galindo, the genial manager of the Concord Mercantile Company, was observed one day this week to be in a greatly perturbed state of mind. It developed that the cause of this was that Mr. Galindo had just had a heated argument with Mr. E. L. Hiteman, who represents the Diamond Rubber Company in this territory."

Hiteman said his tires would add at least 12 percent to the horsepower of any automobile and save 25 percent in gasoline and oil consumption.

"Mr. Galindo does not believe this can be done and emphatically said so in as many words. However, Hiteman insists in showing Mr. Galindo, who insists on being shown; consequently, the gentlemen have arranged to make a comparison test of the regular fabric tires and the Silvertown Cord tires next Monday afternoon, May 5, to settle the discussion as well as to decide the wager."

The two decided to make the test in J. A. Lavazolla's new E.M.F. Studebaker on the Willow Pass hill just outside town. First, the fabric tires were tested with four passengers in the automobile, and then the Silvertown cords were tested with five people in the car.

"The start was made from the bottom of the hill on the high gear with the speedometer registering 35 miles per hour and without shifting gears or throttle. About 1,200 feet was climbed before the steep grade stalled the engine."

The spot on the hill was marked and the Silvertowns were applied to the rims.

"The same test was made as before. The car was able to proceed two-tenths of a mile further up the hill before stalling. Taking this and the angle of the road into consideration, the Silvertown Cord tires showed an increase in engine pull or horsepower of considerably more than 15 percent.

"From standing start with a dead engine from about the middle of the hill, the car coasted 900 feet farther on the Cord tires than it did on the regular tires.

"Mr. Galindo is greatly pleased with the wonderful showing made and decided to secure the local agency for these tires."

Shell Oil Chooses Martinez

IN 1914 THE *Courier Journal*, serving Walnut Creek and Danville, was not above printing rumors.

"Parties at present unknown have secured options on 400 acres of choice land near Martinez for the purpose of building an immense refinery, so rumor has it."

On February 21 the paper reported that either Royal Dutch Shell or Balfour-Guthrie interests were looking at the Frazer ranch property east of Martinez for building a "mammoth refinery" to rival the one built by Standard Oil in Richmond.

Two weeks later, the paper noted that construction of the refinery near Martinez, "presumably by Shell," would put 1,500 men to work initially. Once the plant was built, it would have a permanent work force of 600.

Martinez was the ideal spot, because it had what refiners needed to bring in ships—deep water—says Martinez historian Charlene Perry.

Shell had already acquired a storage facility at the water's edge in 1913. And before the spring of 1914 was ended, company representatives led by J. C. Van Eck paid $144,000 for 368 acres of grazing land next to the American Gasoline Co. water terminal. Construction started on the refinery in July.

When industries came to town there weren't enough Martinez workers or houses for the workers, says Perry. When Mountain Copper Co. located outside Martinez five years earlier, it imported 100 new residents and built homes for them.

The Tidewater refinery had already located further to the east, where the Tosco refinery is now. With the coming of Shell, tent camps were set up after the hotels and boardinghouses were overwhelmed by new residents.

"The town just burgeoned," Perry says.

The Martinez Hotel, built in 1887 at Main and Ferry streets, was completely refurbished in 1916 to cater to Shell's higher

The Shell Oil refinery at Martinez, about 1915.

management. Tea dances on the hotel roof added a certain elegance to local society.

Shell's British and Dutch executives also brought their love of tennis, and Martinez soon had its first courts.

Relations between management and workers were more formal in the early days. No one addressed the manager by his first name.

"It was only 'Joe' behind his back. Otherwise it was 'Mr. Van Senden,'" says Frank "Red" Harrow, who started at Shell in 1920 when he was 15.

"They weren't very sociable in those days. Very formal. They (the executives) lived up there on Shell hill in company houses. They didn't even stop in and visit each other."

Middle management stayed at the new Oehm Hotel, which later became the Travelers Hotel, on Alhambra Avenue.

Walter Pistochini's family operated the 20-room Italian Hotel.

"Mostly bachelors came to live there," he said. "I remember the pile drivers when Shell came in 1915. They were the men who put in the wharfs. They came from San Francisco."

Many boarders were Italians, who played "pedro" in the hotel cardroom, next to the saloon.

There was a big boiler fueled by coal in the hotel kitchen. Tons of coal were ordered every month. It was "quite a job" to keep the fires going, Pistochini said.

Cooking started early in the morning and continued all day. Boarders also got a brown-bag lunch to take to work.

It seemed that every family in Martinez had someone working at Shell, says Harrow. He got a job as a messenger. His father got work as a guard and his sister worked in the laboratory.

Every Friday from 1 to 4:30 p.m., all Shell employees under 18 who hadn't finished school were taken to Alhambra High School.

"There was six of us that had to go. No playing hooky either. The company paid you for that time. You could take what you wanted. I tried to stay with mathematics," said Harrow.

He earned $50 a month for carrying messages on a bicycle from the dock to the offices to the store house during those first years.

"It was quite a bit of money for those days. At the Italian Hotel and Della Rosa's they used to have family-style dinners on Sunday. You got everything—pot roast, chicken, spaghetti, soup, all for 50 cents. They put everything out on a long table and you helped yourself."

Harrow saved his money until he was able to buy a car, a Model T Ford.

"But even then I walked to work. Most everybody did. Some came with horses and buggies. There was a place by the north gate, a little corral where you could put your horse. Everybody didn't have a car in those days."

Horses were used to haul materials around the refinery those first years.

"They had a barn," Harrow said. "The team drivers had to brush the horses off and put the harnesses on every morning."

Harrow worked for Shell for 49 years and four months. By the time he retired as company storekeeper, in 1969, he could call the boss by his first name.

Battles of the County Seat

MANY PEOPLE in Contra Costa County could hardly believe their ears that summer in 1900 when they first heard that Concord was mounting a campaign to steal the county seat from Martinez.

"The little farming hamlet of Concord is not even an incorporated city. . . . It doesn't have a sewer," editorialized the Martinez hometown paper, the *Contra Costa Gazette*.

The *Pinole Times* said:

"It (Concord) is a nice quiet town, and an excellent place to go if you want a rest cure, but it is not our choice for the county seat."

Those sentiments didn't seem to make an impression on A. W. Maltby, former Chicago hotel man turned Concord rancher. He had dreams, and they included making Concord the county seat.

Maltby, a native of England, always wanted to own a ranch out west. In 1899, at the age of 40, he swapped his Chicago hotel for a parcel of Concord land owned by Sam Hopkins. He also bought the adjoining property owned by Concepcion Soto, daughter of Salvio Pacheco, amassing 800 acres in all—and then with his family, Maltby moved west.

He had only been in town a year when he realized there had to be a better way to get crops to Oakland than with horse and wagon. He envisioned an electric railroad piercing the Oakland-Berkeley Hills and stretching into central Contra Costa. If Concord was the county seat, it would be easier to get backers.

An event in Martinez boosted Maltby's idea. The 46-year-old county courthouse was in sad shape. Six successive grand juries had condemned the brick building. In the spring of 1900, $100,000 was voted for a new building.

Maltby reasoned that since the county was going to build a new courthouse anyway, why not put it in Concord—the center of the county. He offered 10 acres as a site for the new courthouse, and put up $5,000 in cash.

Concord Justice of the Peace J. J. Burke, olive grower J. F.

Busey, blacksmith Joseph Boyd, and rancher Robert Caven helped circulate petitions, collecting the 1,792 signatures needed to get the measure on the ballot.

The group promised to put up between $25,000 and $50,000 to help pay for the new building.

The supervisors accepted the petitions and set the election for November 1900—to coincide with the presidential election.

Martinez attorney W. S. Tinning cried foul, claiming that some signers had registered after the petition had been filed. In other cases the same person had done all the signing for the different members of his family. Two hundred of the signatures shouldn't be counted, said Tinning.

Burke argued that the supervisors didn't have the authority to pull the issue from the ballot. Only the courts had that power, he said.

After two months of controversy and a hearing that lasted into the evening, the Concord group suddenly withdrew its petition. The very next day Burke had 16 men on the streets collecting signatures all over again. Within 10 days enough signatures had been collected. The supervisors voted again to put the measure on the ballot.

The new county courthouse in Martinez, at left, under construction in 1902. At the right, the old courthouse—from the county's Classical Age.

The editor of the *Contra Costa Gazette* was horrified.

"Do you want increased taxes? Do you want to see the county seat removed from the most central place in the county? Do you want to incommode yourself for the next 50 years? . . . Do you want the money of the county to be used for the advantage of the people of Alameda County?"

The *Gazette* reported that Concord businessmen had met with the Merchants Exchange of Oakland.

They (Concord businessmen) promised that if the county seat was removed to Concord, fine roads would be built to the county line, and everything done that would help divert the trade of Contra Costa to Oakland.

The *Gazette* was scornful of Maltby's gift of land. It reported on good authority that the offer had dwindled from the original 10 acres to three acres.

"This small tract of land of three acres is valued by the real estate boomers of Concord at $10,000, but any one can go into the open market at any other time and buy it for at least $500," the paper wrote.

The Martinez paper scoffed at the idea of an electric railroad. It predicted that if it came to pass, Contra Costans would have to pay the $400,000 it would cost.

"Every sensible person will naturally refuse to vote for such a proposition. They do not want additional burdens placed on the shoulders of themselves, their children or their children's children."

On November 6, the men in Contra Costa County trooped to the polls. The women stayed home. They didn't have the vote yet. The *Gazette* announced the vote—2,112 for Martinez and 1,223 for Concord.

Maltby, however, didn't give up on the electric railway. On January 13, 1909, Maltby headed a list of the eight men who put $2 million together and incorporated the Oakland, Antioch and Eastern Railway.

On September 3, 1913 the first electric trains rolled from Sacramento through Concord to Oakland. Martinez was not part of the system.

Bay Point Shipyard Hires Teens

WORD HAD GOTTEN AROUND Danville High School in the summer of 1918 that jobs could be had for the asking at the new Bay Point (Port Chicago) shipyard.

Paul Ogden was only 15, but that didn't stop him. He got on the train at Saranap and joined shipyard workers who were commuting from Oakland to Bay Point. All the students who rode on the train with Ogden that day were hired, he remembered.

In 1988, the late Paul Ogden, who was then living in Walnut Creek, recalled that no one thought much about child labor laws in those days.

"The ones (students) who knew somebody got the cushy jobs like shipfitters helpers. They didn't even get their hands dirty."

Ogden became a driller's helper, working at the bottom of the ships below the riveters on the deck. One of the red hot rivets hit Ogden on the head.

"Set my hair on fire."

He also suffered a cut.

"Cliff Thompson was the first aid man. He became the mayor of Walnut Creek. Bandaged me up."

Ogden got 50 cents an hour all summer, working 8 hours Monday through Friday and four hours on Saturday. The pay was great, he said.

"Got our full paychecks too, no such thing as withholding. I earned a couple of hundred dollars that summer."

Walnut Creek land developer Robert N. Burgess was responsible for bringing the shipyard to Bay Point. When the United States entered the war, in 1917, Burgess went to Washington, D.C., and returned with a $20 million contract to build 10 steel cargo-carrying steamers, 9,400 tons each.

He built the yard a little west of Bay Point at Seal Bluff landing where three railroads, the Southern Pacific, the Santa Fe, and the Oakland, Antioch & Eastern crossed the property. Construction on the yard started in January 1918. Besides the four 500-foot-long launching ways, the yard had a fitting out wharf, where the superstructure would be added. There was a two-story plating shed, an acetylene plant, powder house, planning mill, oil tanks, a hospital, cafeteria, and fresh water tanks and bay water tanks.

There were too few houses in the area for the 4,000 shipyard workers. As an incentive to encourage men from the west side of the hills to apply, shipyard workers rode free on trains coming from Oakland.

The *Concord Transcript* saw the shipyard as a great opportunity for the little community. On its front pages it urged investors to build cottages for the shipyard workers in the city, claiming the rentals would bring "good returns."

Not enough people invested, and it was decided to build a new town of 103 houses and a 120-room hotel outside the shipyard. It was called Clyde. The U.S. Emergency Fleet Corporation held the $750,000 mortgage.

The first ship, the *Diablo*, slid off the launch way on November 30, 1918, three weeks after World War I ended.

Government officials scoffed at the rumor that the yard would close before the 10 steel ships contracted for by the government were completed. E. A. West, head of the U.S. Trans-

The *Cansunset* slides down the ways in 1918 at the Bay Point shipyard of the Pacific Coast Shipbuilding Co.

portation and Housing Department, said that the shipyard was a "permanent institution."

"The Bay Point yard will be in operation with constantly increasing activity for at least 10 years to come," he said.

West offered Clyde as proof of his statement.

"Uncle Sam has already taken a mortgage of $750,000 and intends to double that sum. We all know Uncle Sam does not lay out money on temporary fly-by-night security," he said.

At the *Diablo's* launching, Burgess said work would continue without letup, asserting that there was a big future for the yard and its 4,000 employees. The second ship, the *Cansumset*, was launched on March, 30, 1919. After the launching ceremonies, the guests met at the Clyde Hotel for lunch.

In May another ship was launched and the superstructure on the *Diablo* was finally finished. It was assigned by the U.S. Shipping Board to the Pacific Mail Steamship Company to carry cargo to the Far East.

Shipbuilding was interrupted in October when 50,000 shipyard workers went on strike statewide after the Shipping Board revoked a promised raise of 64 cents a day. Some of the shipyard workers went to work in the vineyards and in the almond and walnut groves during the strike. Others moved away, according to the *Transcript*.

The strike was settled by the end of November 1919, and ships again began to slide off the launching ways.

By November 1920 it was clear that the government had contracted for too many ships for the American Merchant Marine. There weren't enough cargoes to haul. The U.S. Shipping Board ordered that four new steel ships be towed to the mud banks of Benicia for storage. One of the ships was the *Mohinkis*, a steamer built at Bay Point for a cost of $2 million. By January 1921 there were 20 ships stored in the mud flats. On May 28, 1921 the Bay Point yard closed after the 10th ship contracted by the government was completed.

The idle fleet of ships was to rest in the mud flats of Benicia until 1928, when the vessels were sold to private owners to be refurbished.

Baseball Summers

IF IT WAS SUNDAY AND IT WAS SUMMER, the baseball field was the place to be in Concord.

Louis Ferreira was 12 years old in 1926, when ballplayers from Concord, Martinez, Pittsburg, Antioch, and Richmond formed the Three C League. Ferreira, who lived in Concord all his life, reminisced about Concord's long-running love affair with the all-American sport—in 1988, a short time before he died.

Ballplayers got together in 1926 and scraped a piece of land on Cowell Road (near the present-day BART tracks) to make a ball field.

"I think it belonged to Mr. Crenna. It wasn't level. There was this kind of a knob in the back of it. They drug the field with a couple of horses. Nobody had grass, and just before the game the fire department would come over and sprinkle it.

"It was a very fast field, real fast, but kind of hard when you fell," said Lou Ferreira.

It wasn't the county's first league. Players in the county had been getting together in leagues since before World War I. Ruth Galindo of Concord said that her father, Fred Galindo, played on two Antioch teams in the early 1900s.

Ernie Mangini of Rossmoor said that his father played for the Pacheco All Stars in 1903.

"He was a catcher—very, very good. He could have been a professional. I have his mitt."

It wasn't difficult to find a place to play ball in Concord in those days. There was always a farmer willing to lend a piece of ground. The players, fans, and sponsors put up the stands, fences, and backstops. Once in a while the farmer would want his field back, and the team would have to move.

Ferreira called the players on the 1926 team "magnificent."

"They could of played in the majors. Coco Commozzi played shortstop. He was one of the best. Slick. And there was Poly Northcutt in right field—could he get around."

**Everyone dressed up to go to ball games in Concord in the years before
World War I. The Concord team's photo may have been taken in 1913 or 1914.**

The weekly *Concord Transcript* usually reported Sunday afternoon games on the front page the following Thursday.

On April 1, 1926, the *Transcript* wrote:

"Northcutt was the star slugger for the locals. He hit a single,
double and a triple and fielded faultlessly. Once he struck the
fence with such force as to cause him to turn a somersault and for
a moment lost consciousness, but undaunted he went at it again."

Northcutt starred, but the home team lost the exhibition game
with Modesto by a 3-to-1 score.

In the 1930s, every major manufacturing plant in the county
seemed to have a baseball team. Ferreira, who worked at the Shell
Oil refinery in Martinez, says a good ballplayer could always get
a good job—even in the Depression.

Mangini played second base and third base for local teams
from the late 1920s through the 1930s.

"Pop Roberts would come out and cheer everybody on. Mrs.
Hammond would make tamales for the players to munch."

Ferreira remembered Roberts too.

"Old man Roberts. He was a rabble-rouser, a star heckler. I can see him with that little cigar of his. The opposition used to hate him. He was almost as good as Mamie Josephs from Rodeo. Boy, was she a squawker. She'd get in the stands and rattle everybody."

The players on the Concord team were local for the most part, but every once in a while someone was lured from another town.

"Ringers," says Ferreira.

"Cano, I don't remember his first name. He was a hot pitcher, came from Oakland, a ringer. He was kind of a scowling type. Chewed tobacco. He'd spit in the middle of his glove, and rub his ball in it and let it fly. He was something else."

Mangini said it was quite common to hire pitchers in the Three C League.

"You brought in a pitcher, paid him $10. That was big money."

Umpires would also get paid. Someone would pass the hat every game.

"My father, Dominick, used to come out and umpire every Sunday. Usually there was just the one umpire, right behind home plate," said Mangini.

Men came to watch dressed up in suits and ties, and women wore hats.

"You never saw men in their work clothes on Saturday or Sunday," Ferreira says. "Even when they just came down to the park (Todos Santos Plaza) and sat around and had a beer or a glass of wine. Everybody looked gentlemanly in those days. Don't know why it happened that everybody got sloppier and sloppier."

According to articles in the *Transcript,* a person would have to be very mean-spirited not to support their team at home. Several hundred people showed up at every game.

A September 1916 game between Pittsburg and Concord drew close to 1,000 people. Concord fans boarded the Oakland and Antioch Electric Railway to attend the game. They even hired a band to go along.

"In those days you didn't have all this television," Mangini says. "The games were always a big thing. You got dressed up on Sunday, went to the games. There wasn't anything else to do."

Cement Dust and Prunes

A 235-FOOT SMOKESTACK towering over a Concord development is the only thing left of a multimillion-dollar plant that could turn out 5,000 barrels of cement a day.

"It ran 24 hours a day," remembered the late Louie Ferreira of Concord, in 1988. He spent his early years in the company town of Cowell, and his first job out of Mt. Diablo High School was at the plant.

"They blasted every morning, about 7. The charges were set at night, 10 at a time. Then in the morning they'd go off, one after another. The whole valley would shake. The ground would crack. The wells and streams on the mountain went dry. Got the farmers really mad."

The blasts, which were used to take rocks out of a nearby quarry for the cement, weren't the only reasons the farmers were mad at the cement plant. They had had an ongoing battle with the giant company from the moment it opened and its smokestacks started spewing smoke mixed with dust. The battle took 25 years and two long court fights to settle.

In 1910, after farmers complained that the dust was ruining crops, and housewives complained that they couldn't hang their clothes on the line, the company was taken to court by Contra Costa County for creating a public nuisance.

The case didn't get to trial until June 11, 1913, and then was heard on and off for a total of 52 days, until July 7, 1914.

After the trial briefs were filed and refiled, the judge finally decided in favor of the company, in 1917. He ruled that the dust, while a bothersome problem, was not a public nuisance but a private affair between the company and whoever owned the property the dust landed on. Then in 1933 a group of local farmers hired a young Concord lawyer, John Garaventa, and San Francisco attorney W. F. Williamson to take on the giant again.

The farmers took their dust-encrusted prunes to court as exhibits to show the judges just what they were talking about.

The farmers said that the dust was ruining 6,000 acres of walnuts, grapes, prunes, berries, tomatoes, peas, apricots, and pears in the Ygnacio Valley, affecting the lives of 350 people.

Ferreira remembers the awful sore throats he used to get when he worked at the plant in 1934.

"I only worked there three months. I had to leave, cement poisoning on my ankles and legs. They never supplied us with masks. I demanded a mask. And (the plant superintendent) asked 'What's the matter with you?'" said Ferreira.

Ferreira ended up soaking his red handkerchief in water and tying it around his nose and mouth to keep out the dust.

The company said is was doing all it could to control the dust. It pointed out that 225 families were supported by husbands and fathers who worked at the plant and that local merchants needed the $30,000-a-day payroll the company generated. If the company had to install expensive equipment it would go out of business, officials testified.

This time the trial lasted 53 days. At one point the company offered a compromise with the 13 farmers who brought suit. It would reduce the dust by 50 percent. The farmers said "no."

On January 10, 1935, the judge ruled that the company had to reduce its dust output by 85 percent or close down.

The tall cement tower, built to withstand 90-mile-an-hour winds and a force 10 earthquake, was completed by 1936.

The little community of Cowell comprised six blocks. The streets were paved with sand. Each company house had a lawn and a garage.

"We lived in a double-ender," said Ferreira, describing what later would be called a duplex.

"Two families shared the bathroom. It was out back in a shed. There was a flush toilet."

The single men had to live in the company boarding house. It cost them $1 a day. There never was enough food.

"They'd give you three pancakes and a cup of coffee for breakfast," said Ferreira.

He said the coffee was sugared in the kitchen. There were no sugar bowls on the table.

The Cowell Portland Cement plant as it looked in the 1920s.

"I had kind of a sweet tooth. One time I asked for more sugar and the cook came out chasing me with a knife."

In June 1946, plant superintendent Earl E. Barnett announced in the *Concord Transcript* that Cowell Portland Cement was closing. After 37 years in operation, the company had run out of accessible lime rock and it was too expensive to ship in rock from the company's other sources, he said. In September 1946, he explained further, the plant was closed because of the exhaustion of high calcium content limestone at the nearby quarry.

Ferreira didn't believe him then, and still doesn't. Neither did the late Victor Heden, who grew up in the company town built by the cement company and later worked at the plant. He blamed the plant's shutdown on the company's unwillingness to pay a union wage.

Heden wrote an article for the *Concord Historical Newsletter* in 1984.

"In 1937 the C.I.O. (Congress of Industrial Organizations) came and organized the plant. At the time, the C.I.O. and the A.F. of L. (American Federation of Labor) were competitors, and the A.F. of L. controlled the building industry, which used the cement," wrote Heden.

Then plant superintendent William George, working with a few company employees, contacted William Green, president of the A.F. of L., and brought in the second union, said Heden. The ensuing dispute between the two unions and the company landed in court and took years to settle.

"When it got to the Supreme Court of the U.S.A., they ruled that the A.F.of L. had no business there and the C.I.O. was the official bargaining agency," said Heden.

The C.I.O. won $1.40 a day raise for the men. "Everyone was happy. They were going to get $5 a day instead of $3.60. People were tickled pink," said Ferreira. The joy didn't last long. Heden remembered going to work one morning:

"We got word that they had closed the quarry down as they had no more lime rock. They kept closing down each unit as they ran out of the lime rock in the eight bunkers until only the packing house was operating. When they ran out of cement in the storage bins it was the end of the Cowell Portland Cement Plant."

Murder Most Foul

WHEN HE WAS KILLED, in 1856, Dr. John Marsh was one of the most prominent Americans in California.

His letters to influential men in the East helped bring California into the Union. His rancho was on the east side of Mount Diablo and reached to the San Joaquin River. It covered 56,000 acres.

A Harvard graduate, he was the first American-trained doctor and surgeon to practice in California. He never got a formal medical degree, according to Marsh himself, because the doctor to whom he was apprenticed died before the document was signed.

In the third week of November 1867, when Dr. Marsh had been in his grave for 11 years, one of his killers, Felipe Moreno, was tried for murder.

"My name is Jose Antonio Olivas. I know the defendant. I knew Dr. John Marsh. He is dead. . . . He died by stabs received from Felipe Moreno and Juan Garcia. They both cut him. I was present."

Olivas, the chief witness for the prosecution, turned state's evidence against his old friend Moreno.

The 12 men in the jury box had been in the Martinez courthouse for three days and three nights and would stay another two nights before the trial was over. The judge ordered the sheriff to keep them locked up for the duration of the trial.

It was the second time Olivas was in court. The sheriff's posse captured him the day after the doctor's bloody and mangled body was found in a ditch 2 miles east of Martinez on September 24, 1856.

But Olivas escaped and remained free until Marsh's son, Charles, knocked on his door in Santa Barbara, held two pistols to his head, and took him back to Martinez for trial. Charles Marsh later captured Moreno in Sacramento.

Olivas told the jury that he, Moreno, and Garcia had been

John Marsh, about 1850.

cowhands for Dr. Marsh at his Los Meganos Rancho in Brentwood.

Olivas spoke in Spanish. An interpreter translated into English for the judge and jury.

"Dr. Marsh was driving along in his buggy. It was done in the afternoon near dark. I don't know why he was killed, but I think it was on account of his (Moreno's) brother-in-law."

Moreno's brother-in-law, Ygnacio Sibrian, lost a lawsuit against Marsh a month or so before the doctor was murdered.

Sibrian sued Marsh for shortchanging him on work he'd done on the doctor's ranch in April 1855. Sibrian claimed the doctor owed him $1,008 for branding, marking and "altering the sex of the male cattle."

The doctor responded in court that he paid Sibrian $180—all the work was worth.

Not only did Sibrian lose the case, he was ordered to pay Marsh's court costs. Sibrian was so angry that he offered to pay Moreno $300 and Olivas and Garcia $100 each to kill the doctor.

Olivas claimed that Marsh also owed him money and was reluctant to pay. On the morning of the murder, Olivas, Moreno, and Garcia saw Dr. Marsh leave the rancho to go to San Francisco. Olivas said he greeted the doctor and asked for his back pay.

"The doctor said he had no money with him but would pay me when he came back from San Francisco. Nothing more was said.

"The doctor drove along, and we stayed there about a quarter of an hour, arguing about killing him. Finally we agreed only to rob him. I came into the agreement to rob him because we thought he had money."

Once the decision was made, the three rode to overtake the doctor.

"Moreno said to go and take hold of the horse. I did. And then Moreno got down and jumped on the buggy behind. Garcia got down and stood alongside."

Marsh stood up in the buggy, and asked, "Do you want to kill me?"

"I said, 'No.' Moreno said, 'Yes.' Then Moreno cut him, first in the face. Then I hollered to Felipe, 'Stop!'

"Then Garcia got ahold of his coat. Moreno pushed him from behind and Garcia from the side."

Marsh fell out of the buggy onto the ground, kicking. Olivas got off his horse to help the doctor, but Marsh lunged at him.

"I stepped back and stumbled and fell. And the doctor fell on me. He had hold of my head and whiskers with both hands. Then I told Moreno to help to free me.

"Moreno came and stabbed him on the left side as we lay there. The doctor then cried out, and Moreno was going to cut him again, and I said, 'You brute, what are you going to do?' I pushed him away and Moreno made a cut at me and cut my clothes somewhat.

"Then we both got up, and the doctor started to rise. He ran a short distance and fell in the ditch dead."

Moreno and Garcia went to the body, rifled Marsh's pockets, and cut his throat, Olivas said.

"Then we all went to the top of the hill. They got down and divided the money into three parts. Each of us took a share."

Some 16 or 17 witnesses testified in all. The testimony ended Wednesday afternoon. The summing up by attorneys and instructions to the jury took until 11 p.m., when the jury began to deliberate.

By 9 a.m. the next day the jury announced its verdict: Moreno was found guilty of murder in the second degree.

A week later, he was sentenced to life in prison. Moreno served 24 years before he was pardoned by the governor. Olivas was released immediately after the trial, and Garcia was never found.

Bridge Sinks Ferry

SUSPENDED by a wide ribbon of brilliant red, a bottle of sparkling ginger ale smashed against the great steel column of pier 11 of the Martinez-Benicia Bridge—the greatest railroad bridge west of the Mississippi.

Edna I, the Queen of Progress (Edna Harrison of Martinez), christened the new bridge with ginger ale because it was November 1, 1930, and prohibition was the law of the land.

The railroad bridge eliminated the last major bottleneck to trains from the east, north, and south traveling to the Southern Pacific's western pier. An unbroken line of steel rails stretched from Chicago to the pier in Oakland.

Before the bridge opened, ferries carried trains across the Carquinez Strait.

Wrote the *Contra Costa Gazette:* "It is the final link in the rail line by which factory and mill products of the Eastern seaboard and crops of the Midwest plains will flow to the great harbor of San Francisco, the gateway to the Orient."

The paper reported that 20,000 people crowded into Martinez to witness the bridge dedication. Visitors arrived by train, auto, and motorboat. Some came by airplane and landed at the Clyde field.

"It was a big deal," remembers Frank Bray of Martinez.

He was 12 years old at the time. His late father, A. F. Bray, was an attorney for Southern Pacific and master of ceremonies at the dedication. His grandfather, Contra Costa Sheriff R. R. Veale, was grand marshal of the parade.

There were four bands in the parade: the Martinez Municipal Band and the Navy, Marine, and Southern Pacific bands. The Henry J. McNamara American Legion Post of Martinez won the prize for best float. The members had entered an old French Army railroad car they'd borrowed from the American Legion in Marysville.

"The whole town of Martinez was in on the celebration. There was a lot of pomp and ceremony. Sheriff Veale liked that kind of thing," said Ernest Lasell Jr. The family general store, the L. M. Lasell Co., won second prize with its parade entry, a train made of garbage cans. Lasell remembers that it went into the store window after the parade.

Frank Bray put on his suit for the occasion.

"My mother didn't let me out if I wasn't dressed up."

After the morning parade he and Lasell, who was nine at the time, rode the train ferry *Solano* over to Benicia from Port Costa.

It was the train ferry's last trip.

The *Solano*, in service since 1879, was one of two that had ferried trains across Suisun Bay. The two ferries were the biggest train ferries in the world. Once the boats were moving, passengers could get out of the train and walk around.

The year the *Solano* was first put into service, it made about 3,500 crossings. By 1926, two ferries were making 13,000 crossings a year.

It took two hours to load or unload the trains. When fog invaded the strait, about 62 times a year, the crossings were further delayed.

Additional tracks were laid just for the bridge dedication, so that trains could go from the Benicia ferry pier to the bridge.

The Southern Pacific pulled Engine No. 1, the C. P. Huntington, out of retirement to lead the train over the new bridge.

The dedication ceremonies were held on both sides of the strait.

First train to cross the Martinez railroad bridge.

"It was a nice day, kind of windy, but not windy enough to blow off your hat," Bray said. "Everyone wore a hat in those days."

Once the train got on the Martinez side of the bridge, everyone got off and "just kind of milled around," he remembered.

At 2:15 p.m., Queen Edna—the local beauty—smashed the bottle of ginger ale, and dignitaries each had a word or two to say about the new $12 million bridge.

It was the 12th largest railroad bridge in the world and longest and heaviest two-track structure in the West.

The bridge had been built in 18 months, an engineering achievement that attracted nationwide attention. It was the first time that a deep-sea diver had been used in building bridge piers, and the diver verified that the piers rested on bedrock.

The bridge gave Martinez new life. The city had been eliminated as a major Southern Pacific transfer point for more than 50 years. The editor of the *Gazette* wrote:

"We're at the threshold of a new era in community life and the development of this city."

With the opening of the bridge, the Southern Pacific had no more use for the *Solano.* Its superstructure was burned and its hull towed to Roger's Point in Antioch and sunk.

For many years, people fished off its hulk at low tide.

Picture Brides

THE BIG RANCHES in Concord, Walnut Creek, and Danville depended almost entirely on Japanese immigrants to operate their orchards and vineyards during the first 40 years of the century.

The Diablo Valley was a giant fruit basket in the early 20th century. Pears, grapes, walnuts, almonds, peaches, and apricots filled rail car after rail car. In 1922, 250 cars of pears and 40 cars of grapes were shipped east from central Contra Costa County. In 1923, walnut growers shipped 600 tons of nuts.

The first Japanese immigrants were single men who followed the crops up and down the state.

Many signed two- and three-year labor contracts to pay for their overseas passages. Some stopped in Hawaii to work off their contracts before moving to the mainland.

After they had been in the United States for a number of years and found permanent positions, the men began sending for "picture brides" and starting families. The men and prospective brides exchanged photos. They met for the first time when the brides got off the ship in San Francisco.

Yashue Sakamoto, a stonemason, left Japan in 1902 and paid for his passage doing carpentry in Hawaii for two years, says his daughter, Chiyeko Sakamoto Tahira of Walnut Creek.

"It was a kind of slave labor," she said.

When Sakamoto arrived in San Francisco, in 1904, he found no one would hire a Japanese stonemason or carpenter.

"It was racial. He couldn't become a citizen. That was taboo."

Feelings ran high against Asian immigrants. Because of the increasing clamor, President Theodore Roosevelt and Japan negotiated the "Gentlemen's Agreement" in 1908. Japan agreed to prevent laborers from emigrating to the United States. However, the agreement didn't work; the Japanese laborers continued to come.

In 1909, there was proposed state legislation that no "Japanese

Picking up walnuts.

or other Mongolian could acquire property" in the state. The proposal was opposed by the congressman from Oakland, Joseph Knowland, who warned it could bring war with Japan.

The *Daily Gazette* in Martinez editorialized: "If war comes, that wouldn't be so bad. (The United States) should fight the Japanese while they are a weak power. Such a law must come sooner or later of the white men will be driven out of California valleys."

The 1909 proposals failed, but state laws were passed by 1913 that denied the Japanese-born the right to buy property. Congress had already denied citizenship to those born in Japan and China, and the doors to the United States were slammed shut to these immigrants by 1924.

Being denied a job in his trade, Sakamoto went to work in the fields. Right after the 1906 San Francisco earthquake, he found a job taking care of the vineyard on the H. H. Bancroft ranch in Ygnacio Valley.

In 1912, Sakamoto sent to Japan for his own picture bride. He met the ship in San Francisco, and one of the first things he had to tell his new wife was that he had lost his money. The evening before she arrived, a thief found his sack of gold pieces hidden under the floor of his room.

"She used to tell me she cried and cried that first year because she had come on a one-way ticket," Tahira said.

Tahira was born on the Bancroft ranch. The family lived in a bedroom attached to the kitchen. Before the Sakamotos moved to the Pete Andrade ranch on San Miguel Road in Concord, there were six children growing up in that one room.

Besides taking care of her family, Tahira's mother prepared meals for the 50 to 100 Japanese workers who arrived to harvest the crops. Tahira remembers a Model T truck loaded with fish, tofu, fish cake, vegetables, and rice making deliveries from Yamashita's Grocery to her mother.

"The fields were abundant with wild mustard. Watercress grew under the bridge over Walnut Creek. We used to pick mushrooms. Can't do that now with all the insecticide in the ground. You don't know what you're getting."

Tahira walked to the one-room Oak Grove school.

"There was a big potbellied stove in the corner, the outhouse in the back. When the indoor toilets came, that was super."

On Saturday mornings she went to Japanese school. So did Tom Morodomi, who now lives in Pleasant Hill.

Morodomi's father, Frank, was foreman on the William Busby ranch on Bailey Road. Tom was one year old when his father moved the family to the Concord ranch to take care of the olive grove.

"There was this big building where they crushed the olives and made the oil. These concrete wheels, maybe six feet in diameter, went around in a circular motion. I put my finger there. Got it crushed. My mother never let me forget it."

When Morodomi's father hired Japanese laborers for the farm, he always found out whether they could play baseball. Frank Morodomi was the manager of the Concord Diablo baseball team that played other Japanese teams from as far away as Sebastopol.

"I was the bat boy," said Tom.

The team was transported in four Model T trucks, often crossing the Carquinez Strait on a ferry. Tom remembered team members getting out and pushing when the tide was low and the trucks had to drive uphill off the ferry.

The first Japanese language school in the Concord area was in a rented room in a Japanese boardinghouse on Willow Pass Road, between Mt. Diablo and Grant streets. The children, who attended public school during the week, were brought to the school by the Japanese grocery delivery truck on Saturdays and Sundays.

Morodomi and Tahira say they didn't learn much. Morodomi says the teacher spent half the time rounding up the class.

The late Kumi Toriyama was a teacher at the weekend school. During the week, she and her husband operated a laundry at Green Street and Alhambra Avenue in Martinez.

By the mid-1920s, the Japanese community decided the downtown location for the weekend school was too attractive. The children were spending their pennies and nickels at the corner drugstore.

In 1926, 13 parents, with the help of three first-generation Japanese-Americans, organized the Concord Institute. The involvement of the three Americans made the corporation legal. A year later, a school was built on Treat Boulevard, in the country and far away from the temptations of the corner drugstore.

According to the incorporation documents, the purpose of the institute was to teach the English and Japanese languages and the fundamental principles of American citizenship.

The most eagerly awaited day in every immigrant family was the day its oldest American-born child would reach 21, says Tahira. That was the day the family could buy property.

For Tahira's father, the dream didn't come true. The Depression hit before any of his children was old enough to buy land.

"He wasn't entitled here," Tahira said. "He had land in Japan. He said at least his family wouldn't starve; they could raise vegetables."

The family returned to Japan in the early 1930s.

Tahira, who was married, stayed behind.

"If we had had the land, we would have all stuck together," she said.

A Man Called Billy

WHEN WILLIAM JAMES "Billy" Buchanan died on October 6, 1950, he had held the office of county supervisor longer than anyone else in the country. He had been voted in as Contra Costa County supervisor in 1903.

The fatal heart attack struck him when he was on his way home from a board of supervisors meeting. He had been born, lived, and died in Contra Costa County. When he came into the world, there were no railroads in the county. When he left, the county had oil refineries, steel mills, and chemical plants. It was Billy Buchanan who struggled mightily to get the county an airport. And after it came, in 1946, people said it should be named after the supervisor. He didn't like this naming business one bit. But it was one of the few battles he lost.

Buchanan was born on September 11, 1867 in a place called New York Landing.

Alaska had been part of the United States for five months, having been bought from the imperial Russian government for $7 million.

The Civil War had been over for two years. President Andrew Johnson was having his troubles with Congress. Members of the House were talking impeachment.

In San Francisco the strike by 2,000 Chinese working on the Central Pacific Railroad had failed.

It was in this era that William and Katherine Buchanan welcomed their second child, a boy. They named him after his father, but from his birth he would always be known as "Billy."

Billy's parents were Scots. They immigrated from Scotland and were married in Rochester, N.Y. In the 1850s they joined the horde of people pouring into California seeking a golden fortune.

A job loading coal

At first the couple settled in Placer County, where William dug for gold like thousands of others. By 1866 it was clear that the

Buchanans were not cut out for life in the mines. By now they had a little girl, Jennie. She was three. William Buchanan made up his mind to leave the mines and bring his little family to the community of Antioch. He had heard there were jobs waiting there at a place called New York Landing. He got one loading coal on the ships that would pull into the dock at the foot of what is now Railroad Avenue in Pittsburg. The family moved from Antioch to New York Landing and resided in a small house at Second and Railroad.

Billy was born a year later, on September 11, 1867. William and his wife then made another decision. They bought a farm on the outskirts of New York Landing. Eventually the road passing by it would be known as Buchanan Road.

New York Landing wasn't much of a town in those days. Nortonville and Somersville were the thriving coal-producing communities of the area. Nortonville had 2,000 people and carried the political clout of the county.

In fact the only reason for New York Landing's existence was that the coal mine owners needed a place on the water to load their product. It wasn't until Billy was 11 years old that the railroad linking the county with the East was laid through New York Landing.

When little Billy and his sister were old enough to go to school they had to be taken all the way to Nortonville, where there had been a school since 1866.

Billy grew up working on his family's farm. He got to be very good at operating the hay baler and working with the crews that traveled from farm to farm. He earned extra money by hauling coal. By the time Billy turned 15 there were two fish canneries in town, where he could find work—and did.

After completing school in the local area he went off to Stockton to attend Heald's Business College. Then he returned to New York Landing and continued to farm.

It was sometime around then that Billy became aware of Nora Carroll. Nora, who was born in Portland, Oregon, had moved to New York Landing after her parents died. She came to live with her sister to help with her six nieces and nephews.

Nora wants a store

Billy and Nora got married on January 4, 1893 at St. Catherine's parish in Martinez.

Grover Cleveland was president of the United States. John Philip Sousa had stepped down as leader of the United States Marine Corps Band and had formed his own band, taking it on tour across the country. The World Columbian Exposition, celebrating the 400th anniversary of Columbus's discovery of America, was going on in Chicago.

In New York Landing, Billy and Nora set up housekeeping on the family farm. Nora didn't like farm life all that much. She preferred working in town rather than on the farm.

In 1896 Joseph Raney, who had been operating a store in New York Landing, decided to sell. Nora wanted that store. She could run it herself and Billy could keep working on the farm.

She convinced her husband. He borrowed $1,000 and bought Raney's store on First and York streets. A big painted sign spread across the wooden building simply stated, "Cash Store."

In 1900 Billy decided to run for public office. He mounted a campaign against County Supervisor Paul DeMartini of Clayton. Billy lost.

By this time no one was calling New York Landing that anymore. It was now becoming known as Black Diamond. The community incorporated, and William James "Billy" Buchanan was voted in as the chairman of the Board of Trustees.

Nora became postmaster of the town's first postoffice, which operated out of the store. Billy got the Wells Fargo Express agency, which was also operated from the store.

Business in Black Diamond was booming, and it was going to get better. A group of San Francisco financiers led by lumber baron Charles A. Hooper decided to locate their giant Redwood Manufacturing plant on the portion of the Los Medanos Rancho that touched the Sacramento River at Black Diamond. Hooper had just acquired the rancho from the heirs of L. L. Robinson.

The Republicans, led by William McKinley and Theodore Roosevelt, may have been in charge of the nation in 1900, but the Democrats were firmly in control of the Contra Costa County courthouse.

This was in spite of the continual sniping by the Republican newspaper, *the Contra Costa Gazette.* Throughout 1899 the *Gazette* had zeroed in on the patronage doled out by the three Democrats, Paul Demartini, William Hemme, and J. D. Wightman, on the county Board of Supervisors.

Board shenanigans

In May 1899 the *Gazette* took after the board because its appointees on the county Board of Education were trying to charge the taxpayers 25 cents for meals while getting the "munificent sum of $5" a meeting.

But in June of the same year the newspaper really had something to write about. It was revealed that County Health Officer Joseph Breneman had been paying $15 a month out of his $50 a month salary to keep his job. It was an elaborate scheme set up at a secret meeting held in Supervisor Demartini's winery. The money went to the Democrat paper in Danville for its continued support of the three Democrat supervisors.

This was the political climate, which convinced Republican Buchanan that longtime supervisor Demartini was vulnerable. However, when the votes were counted it was Demartini who was the winner. He had won re-election along with the other incumbents on the Board of Supervisors.

It didn't seem to be the kind of campaign where candidates tried to outspend their opponents. In fact the *Gazette* labeled the campaign one of the most economical on record.

"In the Fourth District it cost Paul Demartini $49 to get elected. In his campaign, W. J. Buchanan spent $31.25."

The money was spent buying small ads in county newspapers and by contributing to the county central political committees.

The defeat didn't change Buchanan's mind about entering politics. His hometown of New York Landing, which was now being called Black Diamond, was becoming an industrial powerhouse.

In 1903, C. A. Hooper located his Redwood Manufacturers plant on a 100-acre tract of ground located at Los Medanos wharf one mile east of Black Diamond.

It was the ideal location, according to Hooper. Besides having

Supervisor William J. "Billy" Buchanan, looking prosperous.

access to San Francisco Bay, it was at the junction of the Sacramento and San Joaquin rivers. It had the railroad, and in addition it had the proper climate for drying redwood. Among the company's products were redwood tanks, wooden pipes, doors, and caskets.

In 1903 the people of Black Diamond decided to make their town and name official. They voted to incorporate. Buchanan ran for the town's first board of trustees and was elected chairman, comparable to today's mayor.

The growth of Black Diamond insured the growth of Buchanan's store. It stocked just about anything a person needed—clothes, hardware, and groceries. Nora, Buchanan's wife, not only helped run the store, she was the town's first postmaster. She doled out the mail to the townspeople right from a corner in the store.

When the first telephone line arrived, Nora became the town's first telephone operator, and Buchanan was Black Diamond's Wells Fargo agent.

Supervisor Billy

It was in 1904 that Buchanan decided to try the run for supervisor again. By this time Teddy Roosevelt was in the White House. Steerage rates on ships steaming across the Atlantic had been cut to

$10. Immigrants were arriving in New York by the thousands. Italians led the list with 220,000. Contra Costa County's new courthouse was a year old.

This time Buchanan beat Demartini handily with a vote of 252 to 140. Buchanan resigned his seat on the Black Diamond Board of Trustees, and in January 1905 started his long career as county supervisor.

It was the next year, 1906, that the Bowers Rubber Works came to town. It made heavy-duty industrial hoses and fittings. It was the same year that Buchanan's business had outgrown the modest little store on First and York streets. He moved his operation to First and Black Diamond streets.

Ruth Buchanan, the supervisor's daughter-in-law, recently remembered that second Buchanan store.

"They carried everything. One man would go out through the town, house to house, to collect orders. Another man would deliver.

"The family had lovely living quarters upstairs. You could look out over the river. . . . They built a little brick building in the back of it, small, 12 by 12, something like that. It was the telephone exchange. That's where I met my husband (Warren G. Buchanan). He was working in the store and came to visit the telephone operator."

In 1905 there were only 15,000 people living in Contra Costa County, and the assessed valuation was $19 million. The county's coastline was dotted with fish canneries and explosive-manufacturing plants. There was the beginning of an oil refinery in Richmond.

By 1905 the coal industry that had started Black Diamond had been gone for more than a decade, but in its place C. A. Hooper had installed Redwood Manufacturers, which was to employ hundreds of Black Diamond residents for the next 40 years and more.

William J. (Billy) Buchanan's father never did get to see his son take the oath of office to the Contra Costa County Board of Supervisors on January 1, 1905. He had died a year earlier.

While preparing to take over the job of supervisor, Billy now had to serve as administrator of his father's estate and take care

of his sister and widowed mother. In addition, he and his wife
Nora had a growing general store to operate.

As Black Diamond grew, so did the Buchanan Store. It was
first located at Second and York streets, and catered to the Italian
immigrants. It was there that Sue Boysen, a chronicler of
Pittsburg history, remembered going with her grandmother.

"I roamed around the store while my grandmother handed
her written order to Mr. Buchanan. (My grandmother spoke no
English.) Customers came in to buy a little chunk of ice, for this
was the only place where it could be purchased, or to use the
telephone to make a long-distance call. Mrs. Nora Buchanan
would made the call, for this was the first telephone office."

In 1906 Buchanan moved the store to larger quarters on First
and Black Diamond. By the 1920s this building was too small for
the business and Buchanan moved again. In 1922 a modern store
with big display windows was built on Fifth and Railroad. The
Buchanan family was to operate the store from that location for
the next 26 years.

Scottish thrift

Billy Buchanan brought with him to the Board of Supervisors
his Scottish sense of thrift. If there was a way to save a dollar for
the county taxpayers, it was said that Buchanan knew how to do
it. He earned the title of "Watchdog of the County Treasury."

Buchanan's first years on the Board of Supervisors were
marked by phenomenal industrial growth in the county. During
his second year on the board, 1906, the California-Hawaiian
sugar interests bought the refinery in Crockett. In 1910 Columbia
Steel came to Pittsburg, and with this new industry came the
move to change Black Diamond's name to Pittsburg.

Shell Oil built its refinery in Martinez on the shores of Carquinez Strait in 1914. And in 1916 the Great Western Electro-
Chemical (later Dow Chemical) located in Pittsburg.

By 1920 Buchanan was well-entrenched on the Board of Supervisors. He was elected chairman and remained in that position
until his death.

It was Buchanan who got the Board of Supervisors to put
aside a sum of money each year during the late 1920s and early

1930s until there was enough to build the Hall of Records, which later became the county court house. The building was not only paid for in full when it was completed, but cost less than the original estimate.

Perhaps Buchanan's most visible achievement in his almost 46 years on the Board of Supervisors is the airport that bears his name.

In the spring of 1942 the Board of Supervisors bought 309.86 acres of land from the Hook estate to establish an airport near Concord. It wasn't enough land. The board then bought 24.46 acres from the C. A. Hooper estate and not quite 72 acres from the Bisso family. The total cost to the county was $88,734.24.

Before the board could go further with its plans, the army stepped in and took over the airport—in December 1942. The army acquired another 131.42 acres to add to the county's purchase, and constructed two runways spending, $2 million in improvements.

The army held on to the airport as a training field until May 13, 1946 when the county's portion of the property was returned to Contra Costa. The rest was declared surplus property and was eventually acquired by the county.

When the county took back the airport, a motion was made at a Board of Supervisors' meeting to name it after longtime board chairman Buchanan.

Buchanan protested vehemently. He didn't want the honor. In fact he vacated the chair in order to voice his opposition. When the matter came to a vote, Buchanan lost. It was one of his few losses on the board. The supervisors had voted four to one to name the field after Buchanan. Buchanan cast the lone dissenting vote.

He might not have wanted the airport named after him, but he certainly was very proud of the achievement. In a statement to the press published by the *Contra Costa Gazette* the day before the dedication, Buchanan said:

"Buchanan Field was conceived with the knowledge that aviation is in for immense future development. We feel that its possibilities are unlimited ... we feel certain ... the people of Contra Costa will find themselves in possession of an investment that will return good dividends and an industry that will contribute much to the growth of the area."

In 1949, when Buchanan was re-elected as chairman of the Board of Supervisors, he said, "I had no idea the job was going to last this long." He still had another year to go.

On September 29, 1950 he suffered a heart attack. He had been at a supervisors' meeting in Pleasant Hill when he became ill. He died a week later in Pittsburg, the community where he had spent his entire life. He was 83 years old.

Put on a Happy Face

THERE WASN'T MUCH to cheer about in Contra Costa County in January 1933.

Four hundred poor people came to the county Red Cross welfare depot in Walnut Creek to get clothes, and the Lions service club distributed food boxes to 80 families.

Nationwide, 14 million people were out of work. At the time, there were about half as many people in the country as today and twice as many unemployed.

Things were so gloomy that Harry T. Silver, the editor of the Walnut Creek *Courier Journal*, felt obliged to start a "smile" campaign. He urged his readers to put smile stickers on their windshields, and wrote:

"What better resolution can one make than to smile, than to take life's biffs for the coming year with chin up and corners of the mouth up."

Silver coaxed a group of local business people to make cheerful predictions for the coming year, and printed them on the front page.

Dentist Dr. Raymond Burke said:

"1933 will be what we make it. . . . If we buy at home, American made products, the year will show a steady upward trend."

Grocer Ed Silveria said:

"I feel great confidence in the future of Walnut Creek due to its nearness to the low level (Caldecott) tunnel which, when completed, will bring thousands into this section."

Pharmacist T. J. Wiget was more cautious. He predicted business wouldn't pick up until March, when:

"Factories will then reopen, work will be given to people on the Bay Bridge and business will be stimulated in general."

And Edith Bigelow, proprietor of the Variety Shoppe, said that the country was already starting on its recovery. She could tell from talking to the traveling salesmen who were coming into her store.

Apparently the country needed more than a "smile campaign." In May, Congress allocated $500 million for emergency relief.

By June, President Franklin D. Roosevelt had signed the National Recovery Act. It authorized legally enforceable industrial codes designed to shorten work hours, raise wages, and end unfair business practices.

The act also appropriated funds for public works and guaranteed labor's right to collective bargaining.

Every business and industry leader was asked to sign a pledge to enforce the NRA code. Consumers were urged to boycott businesses that operated without the NRA's Blue Eagle emblem.

Editor Silver announced on July 27, 1933 on the front page of the *Courier-Journal:*

"We certify that we have adjusted the hours of labor and wages of our employees to accord with the president's Reemployment Agreement which we have signed."

On October 6, the *Courier-Journal* printed the names of consumers who signed the pledge to support NRA businesses.

It was patriotic to support the Blue Eagle of the NRA. Thousands went to Richmond on November 3 for the NRA parade and to hear Frank Hollander of Pittsburg, county NRA administrator, talk about the war against the Depression.

On November 30 the *Concord Transcript* was able to announce:

"Over 900 unemployed men, whose names have been drawn from a list of the Contra Costa welfare bureau, started to work this week under the federal civil works program."

Concord was allotted $11,000. Fifty men were hired. Twelve men were put to work building a cedar pergola in the park that is now called Todos Santos Plaza, 15 went to work on the sewer system, and the rest worked on repairing streets.

These first jobs lasted from December 1 to February 1. Men worked six-hour days, five days a week, for 60 cents an hour.

By June 1934 the federal government was spending $30,000 a

month on Contra Costa relief projects, putting 1,500 people to work on 29 projects.

Projects ranged from sewing clothes for the poor to constructing the Walnut Creek water system.

The Federal Emergency Relief Administration changed its name to the Works Progress Administration and finally to the Works Project Administration.

Roosevelt initiated the Civilian Conservation Corps. Sign-ups for the CCC were held in Martinez and Richmond for young men between the ages of 18 and 28. Corps members would get room and board plus $30 a month to work in the forests, watersheds, and parks throughout the nation.

The CCC constructed Camp Diablo on the Danville side of Mount Diablo. Corps members built roads, campsites, picnic grounds, and the rock summit building.

By January 1935 the federal government was paying $15,213 a week to 1,192 people working on county projects.

The WPA provided funds for constructing public buildings, roads, sewer and water systems, and sidewalks. It gave money

In the days when you could still get service at a service station.

for nursery schools, adult education, airports, and school lunches.

It funded art, music, and history projects.

In Walnut Creek it provided $519 to map the fire district so that firefighters could better locate fires. The city had to contribute $140 to get the federal grant.

It paid for work on the Mount Diablo Pictorial History, which today can be seen at the Martinez Museum.

Maynard Dixon, who later became internationally known for his western paintings, was hired by the WPA to paint murals. One of his murals can still be seen at the WPA-built Martinez post office.

The NRA was abolished in 1936 because the Supreme Court held that the code system was an unconstitutional delegation of legislative power to the executive and private groups.

The WPA and the PWA (Public Works Administration) continued through 1942, when World War II made more than enough work for everyone. Work relief programs were no longer needed.

The Carpenter and the Farmer

WILLIAM LYNCH, 19, boarded a ship in New York harbor in December 1848 and sailed away to seek his fortune.

Lynch, one of the first settlers in the San Ramon Valley, planned to ply his carpentry skills out West. But by the time he got to California, gold had been discovered. Carpentry lost out in Lynch's rush to the "gold diggins."

His granddaughter, Viola Lynch Jones, lives in Rossmoor, and has a copy of a letter Lynch wrote in September 1849.

"I bought shovels, picks, crowbars, pans, gold washer, and all the implements that was needed. . . . I engaged my passage up to a small town called Stockton, this about 150 miles from San Francisco. Stayed there a few days and heard all kinds of storeys."

Lynch found bedlam in Stockton. Men desperate to get to the mines were selling their belongings cheap. Lynch bought more equipment just that way, but later discovered the reason people were getting rid of it.

"They have to pack it on mules in order to get over the mountains and their price is from 18 to 20 cents a pound."

Once he arrived in the gold country, Lynch said all he found was rock. He wondered why he had traveled 18,000 miles.

His first five minutes of digging proved to be his luckiest time in the gold fields. He found a two-ounce nugget. Later all he found was hard work.

"I dug on with good courage all day digging a bunch with little success. I passes three weeks in the diggins and my gains was but little during this time."

Miners could make from $8 to $10 a day, according to Lynch.

"I give you my word all those poor devils in the mines have to work for every cent they can get for they have to dig in a solid bed of stone."

A carpenter in San Francisco could earn $12 to $14 a day. It didn't take much to convince Lynch that his future was not in the gold mines. But San Francisco wasn't much to his liking either.

**The original Lynch home on old Crow Canyon Road. From left to right:
Leo Lynch, Mary Norris Lynch, Will Tarpley, and Naomi Lynch Tarpley.**

"The weather here is very disagreeable mornings and eve-nings on account of the heavy dews."

The next year he went to Mission San Jose where he met General Vallejo and worked on a home for him. He also met Leo Norris, the father of the girl he would marry.

Mary Norris was 11 years old in 1846 when her parents, Leo and Jane Norris, left their Kentucky farm and crossed the plains in a covered wagon. Later, she would tell her children about being frightened by Indians.

The Norris family was part of the same wagon train as the Donner Party. But at Fort Bridger, Wyoming, the train split. Some went off with the leader who had heard about a new shortcut, which led to disaster for the Donner Party.

Norris thought of joining the group to shave a few weeks off the long journey. But Mary's mother, who was pregnant, refused to follow the "fly-by-nighter." The Norris family followed the proven route through the Sierra.

The twins born to Jane Norris didn't survive the trip. They were buried by the side of the trail.

Lynch, the carpenter, and Norris, the farmer, met in Mission

San Jose and became partners. They bought 4,439 acres from the Amador family and planted barley—the first crop in the San Ramon Valley.

Lynch then built the Norris family a house out of redwoods he logged himself in what is now Canyon and Moraga and hauled them back to San Ramon over the roadless hills.

Lynch and Mary Norris married in 1853 and Lynch built a second home out of redwood. The couple had seven children.

The two houses are now gone. The Norris house burned in 1950. The Lynch home was razed to make way for Crow Canyon Road.

Jones remembers her grandfather as "a sturdy man. Everything he made was strong."

She was born and grew up on the land her grandfather and great-grandfather bought. Her father, Leo Lynch, was in the first graduating class at UC Berkeley in 1874.

"My father was a civil engineer. But when my grandfather got too old, he had to run the ranch.

"He was a very fine man, strict, considerate, and handsome. He wanted us to dress for dinner. Our shoes had to be laced up. Every meal there was a white tablecloth and white napkins.

"My mother, Minnie Coxhead Lynch, came from a home with servants. Her father was an Army doctor. Imagine how it was for her with nine children. She baked 15 loaves of bread four times a week. She had to iron all those tablecloths."

Jones, a retired teacher, went to a two-room school.

"Four grades to a room. There was a partition that folded back and made an auditorium when we had entertainments. After presidential elections, there would be a dance waiting for the returns."

In 1910, the San Ramon Valley High School was started in what was originally a house. She was in the first graduating class. "It was 1914, all five of us were girls."

Jones made up a family tree with photographs of her grandparents, parents, brothers, and sisters on a poster board for a family reunion several years ago.

When she looks at the board, she says, "I'm the eighth of nine children, the only one left."

Charlotte Tells a Story

CHARLOTTE WOOD couldn't sleep after celebrating her 86th birthday. It couldn't have been because she was in strange surroundings. She had lived on the same farm in Sycamore Valley since she was born, in 1864.

There was something gnawing at her. Something she had to do. So at 3 a.m. on January 9, 1950, she turned on her bedroom light and began to write.

"I, Charlotte E. Wood, oldest survivor of the clan, roused from my slumbers to jot down many historical facts coursing through my brain, lest they be forgotten and not included among the records of this old-time Woodside Farm story."

Charlotte Elmire Wood's parents, Charles and Cynthia Rice Wood, came to the Sycamore Valley by horse and wagon from Marysville in 1862.

"It being early Civil War time, there were many sympathizers with both the North and with the South, and naturally there was a little hesitancy in meeting newcomers, so no one called on Mother during her first six months here," wrote Charlotte.

The winter of 1862–63 was dry, and settlers had to scrounge to get food for their families and their animals. Prejudices and politics were forgotten, however, since settlers had to help one another to survive. "... When a neighbor's hungry cow, mooing for food, stopped at our fence, Mother emptied a straw bedtick to feed the poor starving animal."

Word of the Woods's generosity got around, and soon they had staunch friends, among both Northerners and Southerners throughout the valley.

It was gold that lured Charles Wood Sr. to California in 1852. The native of Massachusetts searched for the elusive dust with pick and pan before opting for the more stable income of going into business with his brother, carrying supplies to miners on mule pack trains.

Ten years in the Gold Country were enough for Wood. He had

married New York-born Cynthia Avery Rice in 1857. By 1862 there were two children, Louis and Libbie.

"Troubled with malarial fever (then commonly called fever and ague), Father and his family were very fortunate in being able to move to a more healthful section of the state. I have heard him say many times that he could not have lived a long life in a climate such as there was in Marysville."

She described her father as a "well-read, sterling man of high ideals, good habits, very particular about our English, disliking slang and rude behavior, kindhearted and generous to the nth degree."

Her mother was a "dear, sweet woman, greatly beloved for her gentle, generous disposition, ever doing for others—the ill, the needy, the homeless."

Charlotte Wood started her education in the one-room Sycamore Valley School in 1869 when she was five. In an article she wrote for the *Valley Pioneer* in 1958, she said:

"Some of the text books of the '70s and '80s were *Robinson's Practical Arithmetic, Swinton's Work Book, Reed and Kellogg's Grammar, Willson's* and *McGuffey's Readers*—some of their morals remaining fresh in my memory to this day."

The Sycamore Valley schoolhouse and desks were built in 1866 by Ebenizer Dole, a carpenter from Maine.

She remembered that the schoolhouse was the center for all important events.

"Picnics, parties, school exhibitions. . . . A literary society, Sunday School, and church services were conducted at various times, and occasionally a Christmas tree celebration was held in this pleasant gathering place. Many a happy evening, even to the wee small hours, was spent tripping the light fantastic to the strains of Walter Gumtau's fiddle, or may hap local talent—guitar, violin, accordion."

The school building had thin walls. Once in a while a woodpecker would peck its way through, "requiring many a piece of tin to stop the unsightly holes."

"Most of the pupils came to school on horseback, on tiny burrows, or in carts, sometimes six or seven squeezed into a rickety vehicle."

Charlotte didn't go to high school after her graduation, but continued her education in San Francisco. In 1890 she took the Contra Costa Teacher's Examination at Martinez.

"Passing successfully, the home school (Sycamore Valley School) was offered me and in March, 1890, I began teaching."

Her salary, which ranged from $65 to $80 a month, often helped her family pay the farm mortgage.

"The fact that all my 31 years of public school service were spent in that same room seems now like a fairy dream," she said.

After she retired from teaching public school, in 1921, Charlotte taught another six years as the private tutor at the Black Hawk Ranch. She never married, and jokingly said in her 1959 reminiscences that Dan Cupid's darts "either missed their aim or failed to touch a vulnerable spot."

"My fondest dream is that my life has not proved all vain —that in its four score and seven years some kindly deeds will leave a worthy impress along my life's pathway."

The old Sycamore Valley School burned down in 1945. When the San Ramon Valley District later built a school, it was called the Charlotte E. Wood Elementary School.

"Miss Lottie," as she was called by her friends, died in 1961, 10 years after she completed "Rambling Reminiscences of The Charles Wood Family and Their Woodside Farm Home."

Sheriff Rousts Bareknuckle Fans

THE CROWD of more than a thousand roared when Thomas Chandler pounded Dooney Harris until he collapsed "bleeding, faint and insensible" into the arms of his second on April 13, 1867.

This was the first championship bareknuckle bout recorded in Contra Costa County.

The fighters, spectators, referees, and news reporters had successfully eluded the law and authorities by moving the fight from San Mateo to Point Isabel, near San Pablo.

Two weeks after Chandler had been awarded the lightweight championship belt and the $3,000 purse, Contra Costa's sheriff began collecting the names of all who had participated.

By the time the grand jury met in November of that year, it had 1,000 names (mostly John and Charles Does) to indict for the crime of "unlawfully, feloniously, riotously" assembling to view the illegal "fight by agreement."

Fighting was brutal, bloody, and illegal in California in the 1860s, but that didn't stop the locals from making heroes out of the bareknuckled boxers.

New York-born John C. Heenan was the first prize fighter to gain notoriety in the local press, according to Bernard Freedman of Concord, who has researched the early days of the sport in Contra Costa.

Heenan's nickname was "Benicia Boy," because he had made his muscles swinging a 32-pound hammer 12 hours a day in the Pacific Mail Steamship Co. workshops in Benicia in 1852.

While the *Contra Costa Gazette* found prizefighting a "brutalizing breach of the law," it printed all it could find about Heenan, says Freedman.

In 1860, Heenan, the self-styled American heavyweight champion, sailed to Liverpool to fight England's champion, Tom Sayers.

The championship fight excited the whole American nation.

[REPORTED EXCLUSIVELY FOR THE DRAMATIC CHRONICLE AND NEW YORK HERALD.]

CHRONICLE OFFICE.......4 P. M.

GREAT FIGHT

....BETWEEN....

Dooney Harris

....AND....

Tom Chandler

BIOGRAPHY OF CHANDLER AND HARRIS.

The Chronicle's First Dispatch from the Ground.

IMMENSE CONCOURSE OF SPECTATORS !

Warrants Issued for the Arrest of the Parties.

PRINCIPALS APPEAR READY FOR THE FIGHT !

GREAT EXCITEMENT

INTERFERENCE BY THE SAN MATEO OFFICIALS !

The Enclosure Gives Way

MANY PERSONS INJURED !

Interruption of the Programme.

Disappearance of the Principals !

THEIR PRESENT WHEREABOUTS UNKNOWN !

Currier and Ives hurriedly turned out lithographs of the event to sell nationwide.

However, the news of the bout was slow to reach Contra Costans. They read the results in the *Gazette* on May 12, 1860, almost a month after the London bout.

The Heenan-Sayers fight went 42 rounds, lasting two hours and 20 minutes. The fight ended in complete chaos when spectators invaded the ring and the police halted the fight.

Both men were awarded duplicate championship belts and toured England together.

Back in the Bay Area, promoters of the Dooney Harris-Thomas Chandler lightweight championship fight never intended for the contest to be held in Contra Costa.

On the scheduled day of the fight, April 11, 1867, the *Daily Dramatic Chronicle* (forerunner of the *San Francisco Chronicle*) reported that 3,000 spectators had arrived at the scene by train, cart, buggy, and on foot.

"At the moment when expectation was at its height and the excitement was becoming intense, the Sheriff of San Mateo County, the bold Lathrop, backed by the honorable County Judge Horace Templeton, Esq., and a dozen or more stalwart men of said county made their unwelcome appearance on the scene of the action."

The sheriff and his men stopped the fight. In the excitement, one of the temporary bleachers collapsed and dumped 300 spectators to the ground. Some were badly hurt. The paper announced that the fight wasn't canceled, only delayed. The bout would be held in a few days in a county where a sheriff wouldn't interfere.

The paper complained that the people who had bought tickets for $5 and $10 each would be expected to pay again.

"Who Gets It?" asked a *Daily Dramatic* headline. The paper noted that $10,000 worth of tickets had been sold "for the great prize fight that didn't come off, and which some people say wasn't intended to take place yesterday. A very nice little pile for someone."

The idea of paying twice didn't seem to bother the 1,000 people who got on steamers, tugs, and sailboats to cross the Bay to Point Isabel near San Pablo on April 13.

Chandler, the underdog, won by a knockout. The fight turned out to be so short that the promoters had to come up with another bout to satisfy the customers. Chandler refereed it.

The *Gazette* failed to have a reporter at the scene, and later supported the Contra Costa County authorities seeking to indict the spectators.

It reprinted the *San Francisco Bulletin's* editorial, which called the Harris-Chandler match a "sanguinary and disgusting combat."

By March of 1868 the sheriff had served 19 of the 1,000 who had been indicted. All 19 pled guilty. Harris and Chandler were fined $150 each. The rest paid fines ranging from $22.72 to $75.

Grangers Build Martinez Wharf

THE STEAM WHISTLE at Benicia screamed and the cannon boomed a 13-gun salute to welcome the first ship to pull in to the new Martinez Wharf.

Dr. John Strentzel, president of the Grangers' Warehouse and Business Association of Contra Costa County, was at the wharf when the *St. Charles* sailed into view that September day in 1876. He had squeezed in among the farmers and other Martinez citizens to greet the ship.

Strentzel, who later became the father-in-law of naturalist John Muir, had been waiting for this day ever since he bought his first 20 acres in the Alhambra Valley, 23 years before.

With the new wharf the county's farmers would have direct access to European markets. No longer would they have to deal with a series of middlemen, each taking a share of the profits.

"It is now within the reach of the producers and grain growers of our county and of the San Joaquin Valley to mass their surplus at a central point, whence it can be moved at a moment's notice to any available market. . . .

"Here the producer can meet the capitalist or merchant as principals in a trade, set their price and thus save the amount of former commissions," Strentzel wrote in 1876.

As president of the Grange, Strentzel had directed the building of the 1,900-foot wharf and grain warehouses.

While pleased that the Grange was able to build the warehouses, he worried about the single-mindedness of the grain growers, who only thought about planting and profiting from wheat.

He warned that the ground was becoming less fertile, producing fewer and fewer bushels of wheat per acre, and called for diversification of crops.

He called on farmers to plant orchards and vineyards on a small portion of their land. Reap profits from fruit, raisins, and wine, he said.

Grain ships were a common sight off Martinez in the late 1870s and 1880s.

"Then it will become apparent how long we have remained in an indolent Rip Van Winkle slumber of grain growing to supply cheap bread to distant nations, impoverishing ourselves for their sakes," he wrote.

When Strentzel arrived in Martinez with his family in 1853, he was trying to fulfill his dream of a home surrounded by orange groves, vineyards, and flowers.

He had a small medical practice, but made most of his money through his agricultural ventures. Whenever he had a little cash, he invested in more land. He eventually owned 2,665 acres in and about Martinez, including his 856-acre fruit ranch in the Alhambra Valley.

A native of Lublin, Poland, Strentzel said it was his father's idea that he become a doctor. Two of his uncles had been surgeons.

However, in 1830 war interrupted his medical studies. Strentzel, then 18, volunteered for the Polish army. When the Russian army absorbed the Polish units, Strentzel went into exile in Hungary rather than serve under the Czar. He got his medical degree in Hungary, where he also took up vineyard culture and learned about the wine trade.

In 1840 he and his brother took passage on a ship to New Orleans. From New Orleans he traveled to Texas, where he met and married his Tennessee-born wife, Louisiana Erwin. The couple bought a 500-acre farm in Lamar, Texas.

A few years later Strentzel read an article on California by Capt. John Charles Fremont.

"The masterly and glowing reports first drew my attention to the coast," Strentzel wrote.

When gold was discovered, in 1848, the Strentzels decided to try their luck. With a party of 135 other Texans, they left by covered wagon. They had a horrendous trip, suffering from the heat and lack of water.

At first they settled in the Gold Country on the Tuolumne River. Strentzel operated a canvas tent hotel, general store, and ferry for the miners. In 1853 a flood wiped out his business, home, and farm. Louisiana Strentzel fell ill. The couple decided to move to Benicia, where they had friends.

While in Benicia, Strentzel took a trip across the Carquinez Strait and found the community of Martinez and a pretty little valley called Cañada del Hambre (Valley of Hunger.)

He chose the Martinez side of the strait because it was protected from the fog and winds of the Bay. Louisiana didn't much like the name the hungry Spanish soldiers had given the place years before, and renamed it Alhambra after the Moorish castles of Spain.

"In 1853 I planted my first orange seed that grew well. . . . In 1873 I realized my dream. . . . We have a commodious house, with pleasant surroundings in the midst of orchard and vineyards in full view of Martinez and Benicia and the two overland railroads," Strentzel wrote.

By the time Strentzel died, in 1890, he had experimented with 1,000 varieties of fruits, nuts, and grapes at his Alhambra Valley ranch, which eventually was left to his daughter, Louie Strentzel Muir, and to his famous son-in-law.

Orinda Sisters Deep in Dust

RIDING BEHIND A HAY WAGON—a dirty, sinus-clogging business—was a common hazard near Orinda around the turn of the century.

"If you chose to drive to Oakland, you'd find yourself behind a long slow-moving hay wagon, which you managed to pass only to find another one. There were 20 to 23 of them every summer morning—and deep dust. Our linen dusters were really needed!"

Edith Miner put these memories in a scrapbook that she and her two sisters made in 1949 for their friend Dorothy Roos of Orinda. The sisters made at least two scrapbooks.

One can be seen at the Contra Costa History Center in Pleasant Hill. It was put together when the sisters were in their mid-20s, and is full of poetry and photographs of ranch life and San Francisco excursions.

Edith moved from Oakland to a 612-acre ranch in Orinda with her parents and her sisters, Gertrude and Anita, in 1879. The girls' father, James Ogden Miner, raised hay and horses.

"There was no transportation save what you furnished for yourself," Edith wrote later. "We had good horses to drive and made the trip to Oakland in an hour and a half.

"What food we did not raise we bought in Oakland. Mail came from Oakland. Later, quite thrilling, by Rural Free Delivery from Berkeley. We only had to ride about a mile to the mailbox on San Pablo Road.

"No phone, no electric light, no refrigerator except as you cooled your icebox with ice from town. A wood stove to cook on, a fireplace in the front room, and, oh yes, on your wood stove you heated your sadirons and ironed your starched and embroidered undies and your long skirts and changed your iron often to keep it at the correct heat.

"You washed with a washboard and boiled your clothes in a big tin boiler. It seems there was always butter to churn or to work over.

"There were busy years. Lots to do. Much hard work.

"Roads to be built, barns for the horses, barns for the hay, bridges, fences, and pastures to be fenced for the stock, mostly horses.

"There were 350 acres under cultivation and the hay crop in one of the best years yielded just short of a thousand tons.

"The hay was sold in Oakland and hauled there in six-horse team wagons. They left the ranch early in the morning and returned about four in the afternoon, bringing their loads of seed for the next crop's planting.

"Dad had three hay wagons made to order longer than the usual wagon used. Each of ours held two and a half tons.

"Day's work began before dawn. The men lighted their lanterns, fed and watered their stock, then came in to a hearty breakfast, and I do mean hearty. Soup plates of mush and cream, fried potatoes, big platters full of ham or bacon and fried eggs, and always hot bread or pancakes and coffee.

"It was barely daylight when they harnessed up for the day's work and, save for the noon hour and another hearty meal, they worked till dark.

Bailing hay in Orinda Park, about 1890.

"On Sundays, they heated their water over their own camp-fire, washed clothes in a tin tub, and hung them to dry on the corral fence."

The Miners also had good times. Anita Miner Macey wrote in her scrapbook:

"Oldest sister, Gertrude, nearly 15, was a good shot and liked to hunt. Quail and cottontail abounded."

Many guests came to the ranch, and her parents were perfect hosts.

"There were quail, cottontail, and doves in season, trout in the creek. In the winter, at high water, salmon came up San Pablo Creek and we had many a 10- or 12-pound fish that the men got with a pitchfork for a spear."

Members of the Miner family lived on the ranch until it was sold, in the early 1920s.

Pittsburg Paradise

LESTER LUDYAH ROBINSON—railroad builder, mining magnate, and financier—had it all in the 1880s.

And he had it all in Pittsburg.

When he died at age 68, on May 5, 1892, the *San Francisco Chronicle* estimated that his 8,000-acre Rancho Los Medanos on the San Joaquin River was worth $1 million.

A New York native, Robinson came to California in 1853 and built the first railroad that operated on this coast, a 22-mile track from Sacramento to Folsom. He became the sole owner of Los Medanos in 1871, taking it as payment for work he did for a bank.

He built a home on a knoll 150 yards from the river, and surrounded it with 100 acres of gardens, finely graveled walks, lawns, flowering peach trees, and almond trees.

He had his gardeners plant olive, coffee, Australian pepper, palm, and citron trees. He built a miniature lake and fountain. Peacocks, deer, and Guatemalan pheasants wandered freely about the estate.

Up to 75,000 gallons of water a day were sucked from the river by two windmills and a "Rider hot air engine" to keep everything moist and green.

Western Union telegraph equipment was located at his ranch to keep him in contact with his San Francisco office and the rest of the country. He had his own private wharf and access to three other steamboat landings on the river front. Trains arrived three times a day from San Francisco on the 15 miles of railroad that crossed his property.

Robinson's fortunes started going downhill when he lost a court fight he was leading for the hydraulic miners against the farmers. Hydraulic mining was outlawed, and a judge closed down Robinson's North Bloomfield Hydraulic Mine in 1884.

However, Robinson still thought he could recoup some losses by mining coal on his own ranch, which bordered the Black Diamond Mines.

**Lumber baron Charles A. Hooper acquired
Rancho Los Medanos from Robinson's heirs.**

"Coal for power is cheap. Labor is abundant, living is also cheap and the location is exceptionally healthy," he wrote to W. H. Youel, a Los Angeles businessman, on March 27, 1885.

An accident eight months later might have changed Robinson's mind about the ranch. A bachelor, Robinson had made a home for his widowed sister and her only daughter, Tot Cutter.

There was a fine sandy beach in front of the estate where Robinson had built a "splendid bathing house," according to the *Antioch Ledger* in July of 1886.

Tot Cutter, 23, "a novice in the art of swimming, advanced a step too far from shore and stepped off the sloping beach to a deep channel."

She panicked and fought off attempts to save her by ranch vaquero James Wood. Both Cutter and Wood drowned, while Robinson, his sister, and Cutter's friend, Ella Smith, watched helplessly from the beach.

A few months later, Robinson tried to sell the ranch, but there were no buyers. In 1890 he went to New York on business and caught the flu.

He never recovered, spending the last 1½ years of life confined to bed.

On October 7, 1891, Robinson must have realized that death was near. He picked up his pen and wrote a will, leaving Los Medanos to his sister. He never mentioned his four brothers or his 92-year-old mother.

Robinson usually only spent summers at the ranch, but in March 1892 he went several months early, hoping that the "healthful air" would help. It didn't. He died a month and a half later. His doctors had been treating him for kidney disease.

Robinson's estate was saddled with debts, and at the time of his death, Los Medanos was heavily mortgaged. In addition, his brothers and nephews challenged the will. By the time his sister settled with the attorneys who defended challenges to the will and paid Robinson's debts and doctor bills, the ranch and Robinson's fortune were gone.

The bank that held the mortgage on the ranch forced a foreclosure. It was sold for a fraction of what it was worth to C. A. Hooper, who in turn sold portions to a steel company. The site of the house and gardens is now covered by the USS-POSCO steel plant.

"His death was not entirely unexpected," Robinson's obituary in the *Antioch Ledger* said. The paper called Robinson an intellectual giant with the "social reputation of a prince."

The reporter noted, however, that although Robinson once owned most of Antioch, he never took an interest in the town.

Robinson was asked why.

"There are too many saloons in Antioch. . . . I can never take any interest in the town so long as they countenance the whiskey business as they do."

The Changing Todos Santos Plaza

IN 1869, DON SALVIO PACHECO set aside 20 acres of higher ground near his adobe to relocate the residents of flood-plagued Pacheco. He sold them lots for $1. The design of the new town included a one-block plaza in the middle.

Eucalyptus trees were planted to provide shade. During the first few years townspeople carried buckets of water to the trees until they were established. A white picket fence with stiles at the corners was built to stop livestock from wandering through and damaging the trees.

The trees grew to be towering giants. A well was dug and a hand pump installed. A wooden platform was built. Dances were held on summer Sunday afternoons. All the community festivities were centered in the plaza.

The plaza, known as Todos Santos Plaza, still survives in downtown Concord, although it has had more facelifts than a Hollywood beauty queen.

In 1903 two cannons from the battleship U.S.S. *Independence* were placed in the park. Concord children had their pictures taken on these relics until the 1940s. No one remembers what

The first Concord library building, on Salvio Street in Todos Santos Plaza, was made possible by a $2,500 gift from the Carnegie Corp.

happened to the cannons. But they disappeared during World War II when it was patriotic to contribute to on-going scrap iron drives.

A library was built on the Salvio Street side of the park in 1917 with a $2,500 grant from the Carnegie Corp. The construction wasn't without controversy. Bersabe Pacheco, granddaughter of the town's founder, protested that the land was donated for park purposes only. She took the town trustees to court. Bersabe lost the case when the court decided in favor of the town.

In 1922 the people of Concord voted 86 to 34 to cut down the shedding eucalyptus trees when it was found that their roots were destroying the town's sewer system. But the trees weren't removed until 1929, when the town Board of Trustees gave the Lions Club the authority to take full charge of park improvements.

In the early 1930s it was proposed that a pergola be built out of cedar logs in the plaza. The bark would remain on the logs. Wisteria vines planted along the pergola would make Concord known as the wisteria city. The idea immediately captured the imagination of the town. Benefits were held to raise money to build it.

Ironically it was the Depression that insured the project's success. A federally-funded program to put the unemployed to work supplied the labor to build the pergola. John Hansen, a local contractor, supervised the work.

The wisteria covered the pergola within a few years. People traveled from all over the county just to walk under the lavender blooms. One of the biggest events of the year became the April Wisteria Festival.

Paul Keller, who founded the festival, was the official "wisteria watcher." He told the Concord Chamber of Commerce when the vines would bloom to ensure the success of the annual event. At the 11th annual Wisteria Festival, in 1954, Keller was honored by his fellow citizens.

The next year in April the Concord City Council voted to rip out the pergola.

"It (the pergola) was supposed to last for 100 years," Alfred "Bud" Hansen, son of the builder, recalled in 1988.

However, the cedar logs had rotted. Water had seeped between the bark and the wood.

"I remember we would go and put these support beams to hold up the pergola. I don't think my dad ever charged the city," he said.

The city's insurance carrier told the city it either had to rebuild the pergola or tear it down. It would cost up to $8,000 to fix the pergola.

The council decided to spend $15,000, tear down the pergola, and put in a lawn, sidewalks, and a children's playground. Some businesses surrounding the plaza thought the council decision was a mistake. They wanted to turn the plaza into a parking lot.

The wisteria tradition was supposed to be saved. The mayor announced that anyone who wanted to could come and get a clipping to plant in his own yard. Later, it was discovered that spring was the wrong time to root wisteria clippings.

The little library on Salvio Street was the next to go. By 1958 there was a newer, bigger library building constructed a dozen blocks away. The new library was dedicated on October 19, 1959. On the following Monday the City Council signed an agreement with KTK Wrecking Co. to knock down the 42-year-old building the next day for $580.

"A part of Concord died today. The Concord Library, a part of Concord's historic plaza fell victim to the wrecking ball," reported the *Transcript* on October 20, 1959.

Coal in Them There Hills

THE COAL BUSINESS hadn't been good in the coal fields of Mount Diablo since 1880, and each succeeding year it got worse.

There was still plenty of coal in the foothills. But it was low grade coal and by the 1880s was getting harder to dig out.

As the shafts got deeper there were flooding problems, and it cost a lot of money to keep the pumps going.

The shafts of the Black Diamond mine, the biggest operation in the Mount Diablo coal fields, were the deepest. These shafts went far below the levels of the surrounding Pittsburg, Eureka, and Union mines and thus served as the main drains of the region. In 1884 Pierre Cornwall of the Black Diamond asked the owners of the surrounding mines to help pay the pumping bill. They refused, figuring Cornwall was bluffing. They believed Cornwall would pump anyway to keep the Black Diamond mine open.

But Cornwall already had found a better quality coal near Seattle, and in December of 1884 ceased pumping and closed down the Black Diamond mine operations. The Black Diamond Company moved its railroad and mining equipment to Washington, and many of the miners and their families packed up their possessions and followed.

Not everyone left the Mount Diablo coal fields. The shafts of the Black Diamond filled with water, but the rest of the mines remained operable. Independent miners took the place of the companies. Nobody made much money. Among those who stayed behind were John Ginocchio, Howell Thomas, and W. J. Emerick.

Coal drops to $4.50 a ton

By 1894 the price of Mount Diablo coal had dropped to $4.50 a ton, whereas in the heyday of the coal mining fever it had been as high as $8.50.

Ginocchio, an immigrant from Italy, considered himself a

John (Giovanni) Bautista Ginocchio, about 1890.

miner. But in order to make ends meet, he and his wife, Angela, ran a boarding house and a saloon.

In August of 1894 Ginocchio entered an agreement with coal haulers Howell Thomas and W. R. Jones. For every ton of coal he would dig out and bring to the surface of the shaft known as the Peacock Mine, Thomas and Jones would pay him a dollar. In addition, Ginocchio would get $2.50 for every yard of gangway (timbered tunnels) he built to allow the digging of the coal.

He started work right away, and between August 1 and November 1 he excavated 573 tons of coal and built 55 yards of gangway. According to his figures, Thomas and Jones owed him $710.50. But he didn't get paid.

Ginocchio went to court. He was awarded $532, but didn't get any money because Jones ran away leaving Thomas with the debts and none of the proceeds.

Thomas filed a petition declaring that he was insolvent. The only thing he owned was $20 worth of household utensils and $10 worth of clothes.

Besides the debts to Ginocchio and several others, Thomas owed $49.50 to W. J. Emerick—$49.50 for hauling coal.

Another sour deal

Ginocchio and Emerick continued to do business with Thomas in spite of the insolvency. In the spring of 1895, Emerick went to Thomas and offered to sell coal in Oakland for a commission of 10 cents a ton. Thomas reported the proposition to Ginocchio and both agreed to hire Emerick.

However, that business transaction also turned sour. On September 6, 1895 Emerick was indicted for embezzlement by the Contra Costa Grand Jury.

Ginocchio was the first to testify.

"I live in Nortonville. Live here 20 years. I know defendant (Emerick) about 15 or 17 months. . . . I know Howell Thomas. Know him about 5 years. I worked for him last year. This year he work for me. This year he (defendant) said he would sell coal at Oakland for me at 10 cents a ton. I sent a cart down about 5th of June. . . . I went to see Emerick. . . . He said he pay on 21st of June. The coal . . . sold for $4.50 (a ton). He said then he would collect money on 15 of July."

Ginocchio went on to say that he didn't believe Emerick's story, because he, Ginocchio, had been to Oakland and seen one of the customers who had bought the coal.

"I told him he had money already as I had been to the office, amounting to $100.95. I told him I needed it. . . . Out of $100.95, $6 was to go to Emerick."

Emerick, however, wanted at least $50 because he never had gotten paid for hauling Thomas's coal the previous year.

Ginocchio wants his money

But Ginocchio said, "Thomas and I were not partners. . . . It was my money alone."

Howell Thomas followed Ginocchio to the witness stand and supported Ginocchio's contention that the two were not partners.

"The money from the proceeds belonged to Mr. Ginocchio. I was working for Mr. Ginocchio. . . . I had a partner named Jones, he ran away. . . . I know $50 was due (Emerick) for hauling."

Eight more witnesses were called and more or less corroborated the story as told by Ginocchio and Thomas. Then it was Emerick's turn to talk. He testified that he was to haul the coal, look after all the customers, and collect what was due.

"I am defendant in this case. I hauled coal for Ginocchio, also for Thomas and Jones. After Jones left I hauled for Ginocchio. After Jones left Mr. Ginocchio told me to hang on and I wouldn't lose anything. . . . I had asked Ginocchio if he couldn't pay what was coming."

Emerick's side of the story

Emerick said he was told that when the business got going, the back bills would be paid off. Emerick sold Ginocchio's coal to Judson Manufacturing, Oakland Gas Co., Oakland Preserving Co., and Heckmott Canning Co.

"I went to see all the parties, two parties satisfied. The Oakland Gas Co. was satisfied and was willing to take a car a week; Judson Co. was satisfied and would take two cars a week. Heckmott Canning Co. was not satisfied and asked for bill and gave it and collected. Oakland Preserving Co. dissatisfied and asked for bill."

Emerick admitted that he never paid Ginocchio what he collected, but said he was losing money at the 10 cents a ton commission.

The Grand Jury indicted Emerick, but before he could be brought to trial he moved to Oakland and got a job at the Union Iron Works. A bench warrant was issued for his arrest, which prompted a plea to the Contra Costa District Attorney from H. T. Renton, a land and exchange broker and a friend of the family.

"This is a very pitiable case as the family are virtually destitute. The wife is in a delicate condition with three babies of which the oldest is only six years. The mother who has been providing for them is almost crazed with grief over the matter, and Mr.

Emerick has just secured employment at the Union Iron Works this present week, which I presume he will now lose on account of this unfortunate affair."

Emerick was returned to Contra Costa for trial in November of 1895. He was found not guilty, and Ginocchio gave up mining for cattle ranching, a much more lucrative business.

Cowell Beginnings

THERE WAS SOMETHING about lime quarries that fascinated Henry Cowell. Perhaps he could smell money in those white rocks. Whenever he heard of a piece of land that had lime rock on it, he would hurry off and try to buy it. He gained control of so much of it that he was known as the millionaire lime merchant of California by the time he died, in 1903.

Lime is an important rock to civilized societies. It is used in the making of paper, sugar, varnish, and paint. Glue manufacturers need it; so do the makers of glass. However, in the last half of the 19th century its principle use was as the main ingredient in plaster and mortar, the stuff that made bricks stick together.

If a builder wanted to make a building that would last a long time, he would make it out of durable materials such as stones, bricks, and mortar. Unfortunately, in the 1850s all the lime used in California had to be brought around Cape Horn. Lime was so expensive that San Franciscans built their city out of wood. Cities of wood have a tendency to burn down. And San Francisco did, over and over again during the gold rush years.

Henry Cowell was born in Massachusetts. He and his brother, John, came to California during the Gold Rush. If they went to the gold country they didn't stay long, because by 1850 they had started a hauling and storing business in San Francisco.

At first, John was in charge. Then in 1854 Henry went back east to marry his Massachusetts sweetheart. When he and his bride, Harriet, returned, Henry became the manager of the Cowells' drayage firm.

While Henry was developing his hauling and storage business, two other men, who were to have a major impact on Henry's life, were developing a business of their own.

Albion P. Jordan and Isaac E. Davis came to California about the same time as the Cowells. Jordan and Davis met while working on a steamboat plying the Sacramento River to and from the gold country.

Jordan knew about lime manufacturing. His father was in the business on the east coast. While on the steamboat, Davis and Jordan came across some lime rock from the Mount Diablo area. Jordan, remembering his father's kilns, tossed the rock into the ship's furnace and discovered that it wasn't just any old lime rock—this was *great* lime rock.

Realizing the potential of the limestone business in California, the two quit their jobs and went searching for the best limestone they could find. It happened to be in Santa Cruz. Why the two didn't pursue the Mount Diablo limestone, we don't know. Perhaps it was because kilns were already operating near Pacheco, using lime rock out of the mountain.

In any case, Jordan and Davis found a splendid deposit of lime rock in Santa Cruz, and within a few years became the biggest lime manufacturing company in the state.

In 1860 John Cowell fell ill and left the drayage business to go home and recuperate in Massachusetts. But did he stay there? Three years later a J. C. Cowell was working as a clerk for Jordan

On Henry Cowell's 80th birthday he went up Mt. Diablo with his friends, members of the Woods family of Danville. Cowell is the man with the white beard, second from the right.

and Davis, the lime manufacturers in Santa Cruz. Perhaps J. C. Cowell was John and it was he who introduced Henry to Jordan and Davis. Because in 1865 Henry bought out Jordan for $100,000, and the company became Davis and Cowell. John Cowell's name never seems to show up again in the Cowell company records.

Cowell not only got Jordan's share of the lime rock business, he also got a big prosperous ranch in the deal. By this time Henry and Harriet had been married close to 12 years and had five children. Once he got into the lime business, Henry packed up his family and moved them to the Santa Cruz ranch.

With the profits from his lime business, Henry bought more and more land. By the time he died he had property all over the state of California as well as parcels in Washington and Massachusetts. At one point he owned more than 80,000 acres. Land had to have at least one of two attributes to attract Henry. It either had to be good grazing land or contain good lime rock.

In 1888 Isaac Davis died and Henry Cowell was able to buy out the heirs. Again the company's name was changed. This time it was called Henry Cowell Lime and Cement Company. It had become a big company employing 175 men with an annual payroll of $100,000. A peculiarity of the company was its payday. It only came once a year, when the men were paid with gold coins.

Henry's avid acquisition of property landed him in court more than once. And one time it almost killed him.

On March 2, 1903 a headline in the *San Francisco Chronicle* read: "Henry Cowell, wealthy lime merchant shot by a Merced neighbor."

Cowell had bought a 2,000-acre ranch on the Merced River. Henry and his neighbor, Daniel Ingalsbe, argued over the boundary line. Several months after Ingalsbe's death, his son Leigh continued the argument with a revolver.

Cowell was shot in the shoulder. The wound was called "minor" by the authorities. But Henry claimed that he never felt good after that shooting.

Ingalsbe was found to be violently insane at the time of the shooting and was acquitted.

In May another tragedy visited the lime merchant. His daughter Sarah was out on a buggy ride on the ranch. The horse bolted.

Sarah was thrown out of the buggy. She died of her injuries within an hour.

Henry died on August 4, 1903. He was 84 years old and worth, according to the *San Francisco Chronicle,* $3 million. His five children inherited his estate.

Ernest Cowell, Henry's son, became the manager of the company. He had a pet project in mind. He wanted to build a town, a company town, which would serve employees. He would call it "Cowell." And it was to be in Contra Costa County at the foot of Mount Diablo.

El Cerrito Begins

THE *Richmond Independent* had more important stories to cover during July of 1917 than the incorporation of the two adjacent tiny communities of Rust and Stege Junction to make the new city of El Cerrito.

The United States had been at war with Germany since April 6. Locally, able-bodied men were registering for the draft. Women were working hard to raise money for the Red Cross.

The *Independent* devoted two terse paragraphs on July 16 to the action of the Contra Costa County Board of Supervisors setting the cityhood election for August 16. Getting top billing in the paper was a cartoon and story urging people to raise and preserve their own fruits and vegetables to help the war effort.

During the next four weeks the *Independent* didn't print a word about the incorporation, not even the names of the eight candidates who were running for city council. Then on the day of the election there was a two-paragraph story.

"With a big rally at Davis Hall, San Pablo Avenue, the campaign for the incorporation of the new town of El Cerrito closed last evening. The election is being held today with both sides claiming victory."

The rally included pep talks by the mayors of Richmond and Albany, both of them supporters of the new city. The evening ended with an early celebration of music and dancing.

Apparently there were no opponents at the rally, but the next day George W. Adams of the incorporation committee heard a rumor. The saloon and brewery interests were organizing "a score of paid workers" in automobiles to take opponents to the polls.

Saloons opposed incorporation

Adams issued a statement to the newspaper.

"We have not considered the saloon question one way or the other in this fight. We have been anxious to get fire protection and lights and other necessities and have had no quarrel with the saloons. But if they want trouble we will not back away from it. If this election does not carry, we will try again and again."

While the biggest paper in the area didn't print much news of the incorporation, the people of Rust and Stege Junction didn't need to depend on the *Richmond Independent*. They had their own little publication, *The Journal*, published by Nick Ayers. Ayers had started *The Journal* a few months before the election. However, Ayers was a strong supporter of incorporation and the news was one-sided.

It was the day after the election that the incorporation of El Cerrito finally got the top spot in the *Independent*.

"Hail the new town of El Cerrito. It came into existence yesterday at one of the hottest little vote fests in the history of the county. The vote for incorporation was 158; against 131. Thirteen votes were thrown out because of faulty stamping. Seven were against and six for incorporation."

El Cerrito's first official family, 1917. First row, left to right: George Scott, treasurer; Henry Wildgrube, city attorney; Grace Castner, city clerk; Peter Larsen, council member. Second row: Philip Lee, John Sandvick, Kirk Gray, and George Adams, council members. This photo is a painful example of how politicians looked before they learned how to smile at the camera.

At the same election the voters also chose members for their city council: Kirk Gray, Peter Larsen, P. A. Lee, George Adams, and John Sandvick. Gray, Lee, and Adams worked for the Standard Oil refinery in Richmond. Peter Larsen was a carpenter, and John Sandvick a sanitary supply company employ.

Clubwoman Grace Castner won the race for city clerk, beating two male opponents. With the election over, newspaper man Nick Ayers announced that he was going to build a printing plant in the new town to publish *The Journal*. It was also rumored that El Cerrito was going to get a new bank as well as a telephone exchange.

On the Monday after the election the trustees met at the Fremont school to name high-vote getter Kirk Gray as the mayor. Richmond attorney Henry J. Wildgrube was appointed city attorney with a salary of $600 a year. The trustees also set the salary of the clerk at $50 a month and that of treasurer G. S. Scott at $10 a month.

At the next meeting the trustees thought better of the generous salaries they had meted out to the clerk and treasurer. They cut Castner's salary to $20 a month and the treasurer to $1 per year.

George Barber, one of the early supporters of incorporation, was named city marshal and street superintendent. He replaced the security officer who had been hired by the merchants on San Pablo Avenue to patrol their buildings. His salary was not to exceed $25 a month.

Saloons get the incorporation bill

In addition, the trustees decided to meet every Thursday evening in the Bates Building, which they leased for two years for $12.50 a month.

Trustee Adams then proposed the ordinance the saloon keepers knew he would, a saloon license. The price tab for operating a saloon in the new town of El Cerrito would be $200. Cafes where "amusements" were conducted would have to pay a yearly fee of $240.

For the next dozen years the biggest priority of the city was to pave the streets. The paving of San Pablo Avenue became an issue between El Cerrito and neighboring Richmond. El Cerrito paved its side, but Richmond would not.

When El Cerrito annexed a small portion of an area east of San Pablo Avenue between Colusa and Santa Fe, Richmond officials became alarmed. They thought annexation fever would lead El Cerrito to make a play for the unincorporated area west of San Pablo Avenue between Richmond and El Cerrito. So Richmond made the first move and tried to annex the area in December 1925. It lost the election.

El Cerrito officials then thought Richmond might move to control San Pablo Avenue on the west side all the way to Albany. In August 1926 El Cerrito successfully won in an annexation fight that would put both sides of San Pablo Avenue in its domain. Richmond eventually gained control of the Richmond Annex, but El Cerrito was satisfied. It got control of San Pablo Avenue, and not only that but the state declared the avenue a state highway and finished paving it.

Todos Santos Becomes Concord

FERNANDO PACHECO was so frustrated about the name of the little village, that he, his father, Salvio Pacheco, and his brother-in-law, Francisco Galindo, had just created that he took out an ad in the *Contra Costa Gazette.*

NOTICE, KNOW ALL MEN, AND IN PARTICULAR ALL WHOM IT MAY CONCERN:

That the new town started to the East of Pacheco, in the Monte del Diablo Rancho and county of Contra Costa, has falsely acquired the name of Concord and in reality its true name is "TODOS SANTOS," as may be seen in the County Record. Wherefore, all business men who have any business in said town will please remember its name, and particularly in making Deeds or any other land transactions—for in fact the town of "Concord" does not exist. Sept. 11, 1869. (signed) FERNANDO PACHECO.

Fernando with his father and brother-in-law started thinking about a new town after the disastrous floods of the winter of 1861–1862. The water had all but wiped out Pacheco, the first thriving community built on the 17,000-acre land grant of Rancho Monte del Diablo.

Pacheco, the town, was named after Don Salvio Pacheco. It was one of those bad luck spots, and Don Salvio didn't much care to have his name attached to such an unfortunate place. A fire destroyed most of the town in 1867, and then in 1868 came a 7.0 earthquake followed by another flood.

So in 1869 the three men hired a surveyor, Luis Castro, of Oakland. They showed him a 20-acre site on relatively high ground. Castro divided the acres into 19 blocks of 12 lots each. In the center was a one-acre plaza, which the Pachecos and Galindo donated to the new town. Then in order to induce the merchants to move out of Pacheco, Fernando, Salvio, and Galindo offered to

Fernando Pacheco, pictured with his mother, was one of the
three founders of Concord. He was a huge man, six feet two inches
tall and weighing up to 450 pounds.

sell them lots in a new town, which was to be built on high
ground near Salvio's own adobe, for $1.

One of the first to take advantage of the offer was Sam Bacon,
a merchant, who put down his $1 and bought lots 4 and 5 in Block
B from Fernando. The deed was recorded and a notice published
in the *Contra Costa Gazette* of June 12, 1869. The name of the town
was listed as Todos Santos.

Todos Santos becomes Concord

The three men named their new town Todos Santos (All
Saints), but somehow the name didn't sit well on the tongues of
their American neighbors. The Americans kept referring to the
place as "Drunken Indian," in reference to a community of Na-
tive-Americans who lived on Salvio Pacheco's rancho.

How the town of Todos Santos became Concord isn't clear.
The first reference to the name is a short paragraph in the *Gazette*,
which mentions that the people have chosen the name of Concord
for the new community.

But Fernando still wasn't having any part of the new name. He sold lots in 1870, 1871, and 1872. The lots weren't always sold for $1. The bargain price apparently only was for those business-men who had been flooded out of Pacheco.

The usual price of lots in the new town was $40 to $50 each. Each time a lot was sold a notice was published in the *Gazette*. At first the notices list Todos Santos as the town. The first time Concord is mentioned is on a notice dated September 13, 1870. And then Concord becomes the name listed on the lot sales with increasing frequency, until the only place one finds the name of Todos Santos is on the little Catholic Church built in the 1870s.

Fernando gave up his fight against the name of Concord gracefully. He had a big ranch to operate, rodeos to run, and fiestas to host. He loved to give parties and apparently hated to eat alone. Most of the time 20 to 30 people sat at his table enjoying his hospitality.

Teenage rancher

Fernando was 17 years old in 1835 when his father sent him from the family home in San Jose to Rancho Monte del Diablo. Fernando's job was to occupy the property and supervise the vaqueros. Contra Costa was on the edge of the wilderness. Indian raids were common. Salvio had acquired the 17,000-acre parcel of land from the Mexican government in 1834 to run his cattle. He let his son operate the place and only visited once a year to count his cows.

While Fernando was working the cattle ranch, Salvio was active in the local government of San Jose, acting as secretary to the council and at times as the alcalde. However, war was to change Salvio's daily occupation, and where he made his home.

In 1846, when war broke out between the United States and Mexico, Salvio was the keeper of the public archives in San Jose. A group of armed Americans showed up one day demanding the key to the Hall of Records. With guns pointing at his head, Salvio relinquished the key. With the Americans in charge, there was nothing for Salvio to do, so he packed up his family and went north to join his son, Fernando, on the Rancho Monte del Diablo.

Fernando was now in his twenties and married to a widow,

Pasquala Figueroa Vasquez. Salvio had given his son 1,000 acres of the rancho when Fernando reached the age of 21. The couple built an adobe in what is now north Concord. They raised six children, and Fernando expanded his 1,000 acres to 3,000.

Fernando's hospitality was legend. He and his wife gave fiestas that lasted up to several weeks. Whole beefs and sheep were barbecued. So many people came that the adobe couldn't house them all, so they camped on the grounds.

The adobe stayed in the family until the death of Fernando's daughter Bersabe Pacheco. Located on Grant Street, the adobe has been restored and is owned by the city of Concord.

Fernando was a striking figure. He was big, probably the biggest man in the county. In fact he was so huge that every year he would go to Martinez to get weighed, and the result would be published in the paper.

On October 13, 1866 the *Gazette* printed: "Mr. Fernando Pacheco, when in town a few days since, tried his weight upon the platform scales of Mr. Pons, and lifted the beam at 402 pounds, a gain of 17 pounds within the year since his weight was last taken."

Fernando was so fat he couldn't travel without an attendant. He had a carriage made with a shelf to support his stomach. When he died, in 1884, the undertaker had to have a special coffin built.

The *Concord Sun* eulogized: "The career of the deceased, from his birth in San Jose, has been marked with a series of charities commanding the affection of his entire people and the respect of a large number of Americans. Hundreds of people have been continually the recipients of his unbounded benevolence."

The Great Fire

IT WAS THE ONE SOUND the editor of the *Contra Costa Gazette* had been dreading when he heard the bells of the Congregational Church toll shortly after 3 a.m. on December 23, 1891.

The persistent ringing of the bell could only mean one thing—fire. R. R. Bunker, editor and owner of the Martinez paper, had warned the townspeople only in September of the "helpless condition of Martinez in case of a fire."

The city's water supply had been precarious, disappearing completely in some parts of town by the end of summer. Bunker had urged the town trustees to raise the funds for adequate fire protection through a property tax. It would be the fairest way, he wrote.

On that December morning two days before Christmas the fire started in the Chinese wash house on Main Street near the bridge. When the fire truck and hose carriage arrived on the spot, the fire was still a "diminutive blaze," Bunker was to write three days later.

"With proper water supply (it) could have been extinguished before the people were generally aroused. But as has invariably proved the case there was no water pressure when most needed. It was utterly impossible to make the stream reach the fire, short as the distance was, and there was no way of getting at it otherwise."

From the wash house the fire spread to the Commercial Hotel.

"This was a large building and fed the flames until the intense heat threatened the destruction of the buildings on the opposite side of the street as well as those adjoining. It seemed as if the whole eastern portion of the town was doomed.

"The rear of the buildings owned by M. Lawless on Main Street were frequently on fire, as well as Weiss's and the Martinez Hotel."

The wind had been blowing from the west, sending showers

of fiery cinders into existing buildings. Then luckily for Martinez the wind shifted, blowing from the north, away from the town.

At this point the engineer at the water works managed to provide enough water pressure for the fire fighters. If the fire had crossed Ferry Street, the whole downtown would have been lost.

But even though the town was saved, the individual loss was big. M. J. O'Malley lost his tailor shop and the home in back of it. Joseph Segui's barber shop was gone. It was the second time the town's black barber had lost a barber shop on almost that very spot. John Ipswich, owner-operator of the Commercial Hotel, suffered a $10,000 loss. His insurance only covered half of it. The Chinese laundryman's loss was $200.

Bunker praised the volunteer firemen.

"The bravery of the stalwart band who finally conquered the fire cannot be adequately told in the cold words of a newspaper notice, but they won the admiration of all, and the special gratitude of those whose property seemed at one time to be beyond all hope of salvation."

The day after the fire, Bunker interviewed the boss of the wash house.

"He (the wash house boss) says that at the time the fire started he was alone in the front room starching some clothes for ironing the next day. There was no fire about the premises except the small lamp by which he was working.

"There had been a number of Chinese playing dominoes in the evening but they had all left or gone to bed by 12 o'clock. At about half past three he smelt smoke, and went through the house to ascertain the origin. Finding nothing he returned, and soon afterwards a blaze appeared on the side of the room nearest the hotel and near the front."

The wash house boss told Bunker that the fire had started on the outside of his building. He grabbed a bucket of water and threw it on the fire. He thought it went out. However, almost immediately the blaze started up again and this time went beyond his control.

After Bunker printed his interview with the Chinese laundryman, numerous people came into his office to give him another version of the fire.

"These persons say positively that when they arrived there was no sign of fire on the outside, and that the alley between the wash house and the hotel was entirely dark, while flames were raging inside the house. The evidence of these men, all reputable citizens, should be conclusive. It is positive and to the point."

In January, Bunker urged the town trustees to do something about the town's lack of adequate fire protection. Build a reservoir in the hills above the town and or at the very least buy a chemical fire engine, he wrote.

In February a chemical fire engine was brought to town and tested. But the money couldn't be raised to pay for the equipment. Some pledges were received, but not enough. The citizenry balked at the price even though Bunker pointed out that $600 would have been a small price to pay to prevent the $12,000 loss that occurred in December.

The reservoir idea gained momentum towards the end of February. One plan was to build a reservoir to hold 100,000 gallons, 200 feet up on the hill at the west end of Main Street. The cost of a concrete reservoir would be $400 and the connecting pipes would add another $1,100 to the total.

Fire destroyed half of downtown Martinez in 1904.
Firemen and citizens battle the blaze at the Chaney Printing Co.

Financing again would be through volunteer subscriptions with the town paying $3 per month per hydrant for three years to the West Hill Water Company, which would supply the water.

"Some plan must be adopted and now that the people are in the mood let due deliberation be exercised looking not only to present necessities but to future wants as well," pleaded Bunker.

Town trustees rejected the reservoir idea. The town's treasury was so low that it had to notify the electric company to turn off the street lights because it couldn't pay the bill.

But still Bunker persisted. In May he wrote, "A timely subject of inquiry is, whether all the talk about an improved water supply and a chemical engine was just talk and nothing else. The dry season will come before long and it is little less than criminal to neglect necessary precautions against fire."

In June he wrote another reminder.

"It is true we have escaped a general conflagration thus far, but it has been by sheer good luck, supplemented by the individual exertions of the members of the fire department, now defunct as an organization. With a strong wind no human power could prevent the spread of a fire if not checked at an early stage."

In September, John Ipswitch announced he would rebuild the Commercial Hotel. It would be bigger and better than ever.

On August 19, 1904, the biggest fire Martinez ever had destroyed half the business houses in the downtown. The Commercial Hotel was one of the buildings destroyed.

Giant Powder Company

THERE ARE TWO ROADS that come together at right angles just outside of Point Pinole Regional Park. Giant Road heads south to San Pablo and eventually curves and changes its name to Brookside Avenue. Atlas Road goes east towards Pinole, but never quite makes it.

Those two names, "Giant" and "Atlas," are about the only clues left of the explosives industries that once inhabited Point Pinole.

The history of the explosives industry in California or anywhere else is a history of manufacturers trying to find places to make their products without blowing up adjacent communities. And so it was that the northwestern corner of Contra Costa County in the latter part of the 1800s became the ideal spot to make dynamite.

Julius Bandmann, a well-educated German immigrant, came to California in 1850 when the Gold Rush was at its height. He was 25 years old. But instead of making his fortune digging for gold, he got in the business of selling mining equipment, including black powder, to gold miners. His partner was a young Swede, Henry Nielsen.

Bandmann had left a brother back home in Hamburg, Dr. Christian Bandmann, who apparently had some cash to spare and invested it in a partnership with Alfred Nobel.

Nobel suffered from angina and took nitroglycerine pills to ward off heart attacks. He became fascinated with the explosive qualities of nitroglycerine even though the scientific community had written the substance off as too unstable. Nobel, however, figured out a detonating device, a percussion cap, which could be used to explode the nitroglycerine under controlled conditions.

Nobel secured patents for the device in 1863 and 1864 and formed a company to manufacture nitroglycerine, which he called "blasting oil." Nobel's business prospered from the beginning, so much so that he decided to open a second plant in

Germany in 1865. He looked around and found two financial backers, Dr. Bandmann and Theodore Winckler, a Swedish merchant.

Dr. Bandmann wrote his brother, Julius, in California to tell him that he too was in the explosives business. Christian Bandmann suggested that his brother add the "blasting oil" to his line of mining supplies.

Deadly explosions

In April 1866 the S.S. *Europe,* carrying 70 cases of nitroglycerine for the firm of Bandmann and Nielsen, blew up on the Atlantic side of the Isthmus of Panama. Sixty people were killed. A few weeks later an unlabeled case of nitroglycerine destined for Los Angeles blew up in the courtyard of the Wells Fargo Co. when four men tried to open it up with a chisel and hammer to find out what was in it.

The two nasty explosions galvanized the governments of both

**Burros were used to carry the Giant Powder Company's explosives
to the mines. (This photo was taken at Pike's Peak, Colorado.)
The slogan might be: Don't make no sudden moves.**

Europe and the United States. Laws were passed on both sides of the Atlantic prohibiting the shipment of nitroglycerine.

Just when it looked as if Bandmann and Nielsen were going to be put out of business, Nobel came through with another invention, a "safety powder," better known as dynamite.

Julius and his partner decided that it would be better if they manufactured the dynamite in California rather than waiting for foreign shipments. They obtained permission from brother Christian to apply for patents in the United States, but unfortunately for them, did not get official permission from Nobel himself.

Bandmann and Nielsen formed a new company, the Giant Powder Co., and then built the first dynamite factory in the United States in Rock House Gulch in the San Francisco Mission District. By February 1868 they had made their first 10 pounds of dynamite, which they tested by blasting a 42-pound cannon ball 100 yards into San Francisco Bay from the shoreline. In March the partners had their first commercial run, making 1,300 pounds of explosives in a two-week period.

But tragedy was on its way. In November 1869 the Giant Powder Co. factory blew up, killing two people. The partners then bought 25 acres of sand dunes south of what became Golden Gate Park. In spite of the setback, the business grew and was soon producing 2,000 pounds of dynamite a day and not keeping up with demand.

It was about this same time that General Henry DuPont and his company, the California Powder Works, joined other members of the explosives industry to try to wrench the exclusive patent to manufacture dynamite from the Giant Powder Co. DuPont was successful. The United States voided the patent and now all the companies in the explosives industry rushed to build dynamite plants.

Dynamite making moves to Contra Costa

The Giant Powder Co. was able to stay on its sand dunes for 10 years, but then on January 14, 1879 an explosion hit the plant, followed by another one three months later. The company was forced to move to the East Bay, where they located their plant on what later became Golden Gate Fields, in Albany. The plant at the new location blew up in 1883, 1886, and in 1887—and in 1892 came the biggest blast of all. It was labeled the "greatest dynamite explosion which has ever occurred in the United States," by the *San Francisco Call*.

The contents of two magazines containing 230,000 pounds of dynamite exploded. The blast was felt as far away as Sacramento, and windows were shattered all over the East Bay, causing $25,000 in damage.

The scene of the blast actually became a tourist attraction. The Southern Pacific put on a special train running every half hour from the ferry to the explosion site, carrying some 10,000 sightseers.

The 1892 explosion caused the powder company to move again. This time Bandmann merged his company with the Safety Nitro Powder Company, which had been operating at Point Pinole since 1881. The new company was called the Giant Powder Company Consolidated.

Moving did not stop the explosions. But the explosive manufacturing plant at Point Pinole was so isolated that it was able to operate for 68 years as the Giant Powder Company and later as Atlas Powder.

Isabella and Rafael

EVERYONE HAD TO DO THEIR SHARE in Contra Costa in the 1850s to see that local government worked. Farmers, teachers, or merchants doubled as constables, legislators, judges, and public administrators.

Matthew R. Barber was that kind of civic-minded man. The Gold Rush had brought him to California in 1849, but like most others, after a few months in the mines he was ready to get into another line of work. It was while he was cutting down redwoods in Moraga that his name first showed up in Contra Costa as a government official. Barber prepared the ballots for the first election of officers for Contra Costa County, which then included most of Alameda County.

He then became a carpenter and started building houses in and around Martinez. But by 1852 he had made enough money to buy 443 acres two miles from Martinez and settled down to raise wheat, fruit, and grapes.

Barber had been in Martinez for almost four years when he got another call to public duty. In 1856 he was chosen to serve on the Grand Jury, and was elected foreman. These were the days when it was the duty of the Grand Jury to determine whether there was enough evidence to hold someone for criminal trial. The first homicide to come before the Grand Jury that summer in August was the "People versus Rafael, an Indian, and Isabella, an Indian woman."

The Grand Jury, headed by Barber, listened to the story of the killing of one Terence McDonald, 35. McDonald was working a piece of land two miles from Marsh Landing near what was then called New York and eventually became Pittsburg.

The victim was a drinker

Witness John Crowley said, "McDonald was a fair-sized man, taller than the Indians and a little heavier. He was a laborer. . . a straight healthy man, some times got intoxicated."

According to the story told the Grand Jury, it was late April when McDonald decided he needed help to dig a well for his place. He was looking for cheap labor, and laborers didn't come any cheaper than Native Americans.

Even though California became part of the Union in 1850, the state didn't become the land of the free for everyone, especially Native Americans. Under one of the first laws passed by the state legislature, any unemployed Indian could be declared a vagrant and forced to work for the state. If there wasn't any government work available, the Indian could be auctioned off to the highest bidder and required to work off the debt as an indentured servant.

In addition there were unscrupulous men who made a regular business out of kidnapping Indian children and selling them as household or farm servants.

Rafael and Isabella were two of four or five Native Americans hired by McDonald. The whole group, apparently, were runaways. Isabella had been a servant in the household of Theodora Soto de Briones since she was eight.

Isabella and Rafael had been chopping wood for McDonald's neighbor, when McDonald offered them a job. He would pay them something and let them sleep in his house. It wasn't much of a house, just one room with a stove, a table, a bed, and a couple of mattresses on the floor. Isabella and Rafael would be sleeping in the same room as McDonald. The other Indian workers could sleep in the corral.

The woman was the cause of crime

Some time after McDonald hired them, three riders from the Briones ranch came to claim them and to bring them back to Pinole. McDonald sent them away, insisting that they had no right to them since there were no indentured servants in this county.

The well never did get finished. By June 11, McDonald was dead. His money was missing. He had been stabbed three times in the side and once in the neck. The coroner determined that he died instantly.

Isabella and Rafael hid in the foothills of Mount Diablo with Manuel, another of the Indians who was working on the well.

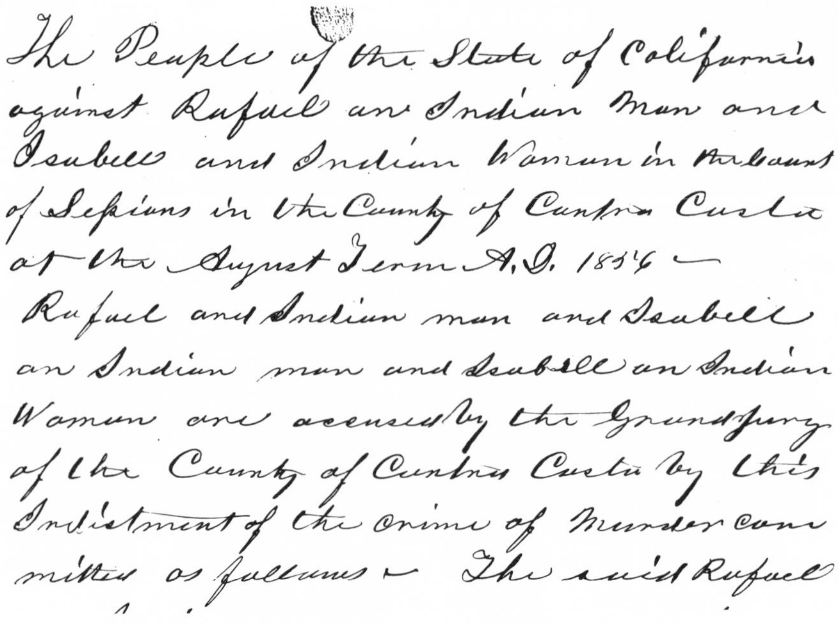

[Handwritten text reproduced below:]

The People of the State of California against Rafael an Indian Man and Isabella and Indian Woman in the County of Sepions in the County of Contra Costa at the August Term A.D. 1856 —

Rafael and Indian man and Isabella an Indian man and Isabella an Indian Woman are accused by the Grandjury of the County of Contra Costa by this Indictment of the crime of Murder committed as follows — The said Rafael

**A portion of the subpoena served in 1856 on witnesses
in the case of the People versus Rafael and Isabella.**

After a day, all three fled to Pinole where they were picked up by the local constable.

The Grand Jury indicted Rafael and Isabella for murder. Judge George F. Worth appointed two attorneys and an interpreter for them. Hiram Mills was the district attorney, and John Marsh the interpreter for the prosecution. The trial started on September 11, 1856. Rafael and Isabella were given the last name of Briones.

Manuel turned state's evidence, and was the first witness called by the prosecution:

"They (Rafael and Isabella) told me they had killed him. They said McDonald was sitting down on a table. They said they were in bed. McDonald got up and took hold of a gun. Then she (went) after the ax and struck McDonald on the neck. . . . In the whole conversation I had with them, Rafael only told me the woman was the cause."

Clark finds the body

McDonald's neighbor, John Clark, found the body. He told the court, "We went to McDonald's house on the morning of the 12th of June and found him dead, the doors barred. He had a wound on the breast, a cut on the chin to the bone. He had large whiskers and a cut on the side of the neck.

"I examined around the premises and found an ax with blood on it, 10 or 15 steps from the house. . . . I don't know where the Indians went that were there at McDonald's on the 11th. . . . None of the Indians were there the next morning."

Under cross-examination Clark said that he talked with Isabella and Rafael on July 22.

"Rafael admitted that he had stabbed the Irishman. The woman made a clear confession. She told me that they were there some weeks before the Irishman wanted to take her from Rafael, that he had a gun in his hand and used threats toward them, that Rafael sprang behind the Irishman, caught him by the arm, and brought him to the ground, and she took a knife that was lying on the table and cut the Irishman in his throat."

The defense attorneys only called two witnesses, Theodora Soto de Briones and Celso Amador. Both swore that Isabella had come to the Briones rancho three years earlier when she was eight or nine years old.

"I know that girl, the defendant. I have known her for three years. I believe her to be about 13 years old. She was eight or nine when I got her and have had her about three years. I don't know when she was born." So testified de Briones.

Rafael gets 10 years

Both Rafael and Isabella were found guilty of manslaughter. Rafael was sentenced to 10 years in San Quentin Prison. Isabella got 18 months. The judge refused a request of the defense to instruct the jury to find Isabella not guilty because she was under the age of 14.

Grand Jury foreman Barber had little time to reflect on the outcome of the trial. A few days after it was over, Dr. John Marsh, who was the interpreter for the court in the McDonald case, was killed by two disgruntled cowhands. And the Grand Jury had another homicide case on its hands.

Albert Stone of Alamo

IT WAS A HOT NIGHT in August 1872 when the members of the Contra Costa Farmers' Club met in Walnut Creek to discuss "The most economical way of conducting a farm."

Nathaniel Jones, club president, was champing at the bit. Attendance had been dropping. Jones was so upset he had written a letter in July to the *Contra Costa Gazette.*

"It is a matter of deep regret that farmers cannot be aroused to a sense of their immediate and future interests. . . . We have not had a quorum for the last two meetings. . . . Farmers, we must protect ourselves from the unjust and unreasonable exactions of organized capital."

Like almost every other farmer in the state, Jones had a major complaint about the existing railroad monopoly. California had been struggling with a depression that started four years earlier. People had expected that the completion of the transcontinental railroad in 1869 would bring prosperity to the state. Instead, it opened the state to intense competition from eastern cities.

Land prices were high. Farmers' profits low. The railroad brought in thousands of new immigrants who couldn't afford to buy their own farms. These new immigrants added to the already existing oversupply of labor. Freight costs kept increasing. The Central Pacific had a monopoly on rail traffic, and in addition had bought out the California Steam Navigation Company, which meant that the railroad controlled river traffic too.

Albert Stone joins the Farmers Club

The farmers had been organizing. Some realized that they needed to exchange information and that they needed political clout. But there were a lot of things to do on a farm, and sometimes a person would get too tired to go to a meeting.

Albert Ward Stone was one of the leading grain growers of the county. He always had something to display at the County Fair—a prize bull, apples, sugar beets, or gooseberries. He had joined the county farmer's club and later would become a member of the

**"Colonel" Albert Ward Stone was one of the more prosperous farmers
in the county during the lean depression years of the 1870s.**

Danville Grange. But he didn't seem to be as aggressive in the
political arena as some of his fellow club members.

Stone liked the information exchange that went on at farmers'
club meetings best. He owned 800 acres of some of the best land
in Alamo. He had been farming in the San Ramon Valley area for
14 years, ever since 1858.

He was well-respected for his agricultural knowledge as well
as for his other skills, which apparently included setting bones.
The *Contra Costa Gazette* reported one such incident in January
1863 when a "Portuguese laborer taking a stallion to water" lost
control of the horse. Besides broken bones, the man suffered
severe lacerations.

"Colonel Stone, himself, was obliged to undertake it (medical treatment), and from the report of our informant must have done a credible job moving all the parts into place and fastening them with stitches and adhesive strips quite skillfully. If the piece of surgery turns out as well as is hoped the Colonel will have earned the thanks and gratitude of the subject (even) if he does not get a medical diploma. At all events his service in doing the best he could in an emergency when no expert was to be found furnishes a good example of common sense effort."

Earns title of Colonel

Stone had worked hard all his life. A native of Pennsylvania, Stone moved with his family to Michigan when he was 14 years old, and later to Iowa. Indian wars were raging in the territories. Stone organized a group of men to fight the Indians, and earned the title of "Colonel," which was to follow him the rest of his life.

He became a blacksmith, and earned enough money by the time he was 26 to take a bride. It was to be a short marriage. Mary Jane Ward Stone died four years later, in 1851, leaving Stone with a tiny two-year-old son.

In May 1852 Stone decided to check out the reports coming from the golden state of California. He drove a herd of cattle across the plains, arriving in Sacramento that September. He sold the cattle, and by February 1853 he was on his way home, sailing by way of Panama to New Orleans and then up the river to Iowa.

He liked what he had found in California. He only came back to Iowa to marry Martha Smith and to take her and his son, Edward Albert Stone, back to California. By this time his father, Silas, also was ready to take on the West. Silas already had moved his family several times. At 61 he was ready to go again, accompanying his son Albert, who was the captain of the 50-wagon train. Silas bought a farm in a little valley in Contra Costa County, which still bears his name—Stone Valley. Albert bought a ranch and started raising stock in Colusa County. However, the Sacramento Valley wasn't a healthy place at the time. Diseases such as malaria were prevalent. Since Albert liked the little valley his father chose, he sold his stock ranch and bought 400 acres in Stone Valley.

Has to pay for land twice

Albert continued raising stock, cattle, horses, sheep, and hogs. But in the midst of all this buying, along came the notorious land grabber, Horace Carpentier. He instigated a claim against the land titles of many of the valley owners. Rather than struggle through years of litigation, Stone made the decision to pay for his land again, and he did. He also kept buying the smaller farms all around him until he owned 800 acres.

For the most part he made his living raising hay and grain. Years later his granddaughter, Friederiche Humburg Jackson, was to remember his four- and six-horse teams that hauled the grain to the Pacheco and Martinez warehouses, some 12 and 15 miles away. It was an all-day, very dusty trip.

His granddaughter recalled that he built a 12-room frame house, a windmill and tank, and piped water a mile and a half across the ranch to a 100,000-gallon reservoir.

He also did something about the education of his children. He and his wife had seven of them. According to his granddaughter, he organized a neighborhood school by outfitting a small house on his property and hiring a teacher.

So it was no wonder that Stone had the respect of all his neighbors. At the August 1872 meeting, he left it to others to complain about the railroad. Stone talked about harvesting wheat and the value of sheep.

Stone told them, "I can take up my grain loose cheaper than I can by binding. I have one man that can average three acres per day with a fork."

Then he spoke up about his ideas on sheep.

"If a large flock of sheep could be placed on land they might clear it of weeds, but if a few run at large on a farm they generally look for the best food."

In the third week of August 1890, Stone took a trip to Oakland. When he returned home a few days later he complained about not feeling well. He took to his bed and died on August 27, just a month short of his 69th birthday.

Martinez in the 1850s

ELIZABETH LAWRENCE was 12 years old in 1852 when she left her native Nantucket Island for a long sea journey to California with her mother.

Her father, George, had been in California for at least two years when he sent for his wife, Emeline, and daughter Elizabeth. Dr. George Lawrence was probably lured to California by the Gold Rush, but must have thought better of working in the mining country, because by 1850 he was operating a drug store, the Emporium for Botanic and Patent Medicines, on Main Street in Martinez.

One of his more popular medicines, which he advertised in the *Contra Costa Gazette,* was "Japanese Salve." Lawrence said it was "the best preparation that has ever been discovered for the cure of poison from poison oak, mosquito bites, cuts, sprains, and nursing sore breasts."

Lawrence, a prudent man, decided that the Nicaragua route to California would be the safest for his wife and daughter. The two would board a ship in New York with a party of friends and sail to Nicaragua, where they would cross to the Pacific by mule train and boat. Once on the Pacific Coast they would board another ship for the trip up the coast.

By 1852 the sea voyages to California, which had taken up to six months five years earlier, were now being completed in four weeks. One clipper ship, the *Flying Cloud,* had made it around Cape Horn to San Francisco in 89 days. But Elizabeth and her mother were to travel by the more prevalent steamship. It was May 5, 1852 when the pair left for California.

Elizabeth wrote that the trip to and across Nicaragua was uneventful. However the party of 1,000 men, women, and children met disaster on board the steamship *North American,* which was supposed to take them up the coast to San Francisco. The ship was wrecked and the passengers were dropped off at San Juan del Sur, Nicaragua, where they remained for the next month.

June was hot and humid on the Central American coast. It was a month filled with sickness and death for the passengers of the *North American*. Although the passengers had money, there was little food to buy. People died and were buried in "rude boxes" without ceremony. Finally the steamship *Louis*, sailing from Cape Horn, stopped and picked them up. Even then the dying didn't stop. Thirty more people died on the last leg of the trip to San Francisco and were buried at sea.

"Those coming across the plains in palace cars (trains) at the present time have little idea of the trials and difficulties experienced by the pioneers coming to California," Elizabeth was to write in later years.

Elizabeth and her mother sailed into San Francisco Bay on July 7, 1852. The city on the Bay wasn't much. "San Francisco was a queer looking place built up of adobe houses, wooden shanties and tents and a few two-story structures. The shores of the Bay reached up to what is now Montgomery Street, and beyond Market Street all was sand dunes."

George Lawrence picked up his family and took them immediately to Martinez. Elizabeth found that there was only one other girl her age in the village.

A "Broom Team"—part of the Martinez dramatic society in the 1870s.

"Martinez seemed an ideal place for a home. The waters of Carquinez strait reached to Howard Street; the Alhambra Creek ebbed and flowed to the town limits. It was nearly full of water all the year around and was bordered by beautiful trees of oak, madrone, manzanita, willow, buckeye, and golden berry, with vines and wild roses on its banks. It was very beautiful. The whole valley was dotted with live oak trees and in the spring time it was like a garden with lovely wild flowers growing in luxurious profusion.

"Bands of Spanish cattle roamed at large over the valleys. One could ride from Martinez to Mt. Diablo valley without seeing a wooden house or board fence.

"It was a pastoral country and ranchers sold hides and tallow. Beef was cheap and plentiful; nearly all other food stuff was brought around the horn. Flour sold in the year of 1852 and 1853 for $50 a barrel; eggs were $3 a dozen; apples $1 each and not many to be had at that price. We could get oranges, bananas, and limes which were brought by steamers to San Francisco once a month.

"Gold was plenty; wages high and there was little or no sickness. So all were happy and hopeful for a bright future. The soil which was responsive to primitive ways of cultivation soon yielded an abundant harvest. The U.S. mail arrived once a month from New York and the postage on a letter was 30 cents.

"There was only one American girl of my age, 12 years, in town. During the fall of 1852 two others came and by the summer of 1853 there were seven girls," Elizabeth recollected years later.

Also arriving in Martinez in 1852 was another New Englander, 17-year-old Charles Carroll Swain from Maine. His father, Seth Swain, had started a ferry business with partner O. C. Coffin between Benicia and Martinez. Seth Swain also had a farm in Lafayette, where Charles and his brother James spent their first winter. In 1853, the 18-year-old Charles Swain was offered a job as deputy sheriff by Sheriff J. F. Smith, and he took it.

The job didn't pay very well, and Swain went into the freighting business in 1853, commanding the sloop *Hudson* and later the schooner *Queen of the Bay*. His boats carried wheat from the Pacheco warehouses to San Francisco for $4 a ton.

Elizabeth Lawrence and Charles Swain must have met the year both arrived from the East. Martinez was still a very small town where everyone knew each other. In 1857 Elizabeth and Charles were married. She was only 17 and he was 21. Swain left the freighting business and went into farming and cattle raising. A few years later Swain became the agent for Wells, Fargo & Co. Express and Western Union Telegraph.

Moraga's Little San Simeon

IT WASN'T DONALD RHEEM'S idea to come out to Moraga in 1934. He had a beautiful home and a comfortable life in Piedmont.

He and his brother Richard were doing well with a galvanizing company they started in 1925.

The Rheems inherited their business talents from their father, William S. Rheem, who built the Standard Oil Refinery in Richmond.

However, they probably didn't inherit a big fortune. When Donald Rheem went into business with his brother, he borrowed from his mother-in-law.

A native of Alameda, Donald had grown up in Oakland and graduated from University High School. He never went to college, perhaps because his father dropped dead in a Santa Cruz restaurant when Donald was 18.

While Donald Rheem may have been content living in what was basically his hometown, his wife was not. Alice Goodfellow Rheem liked horses. She loved to ride. The couple had no children and later she would say her horses were her children.

Rheem acquired 16 acres and a three-bedroom house in remote Moraga in December 1934, and gave his wife the one Christmas present she wanted—a place where she could keep and ride horses.

At first Rheem regarded Moraga as his summer home. But within a few years he spent $750,000 on a new wing, a five-car garage, stable, horse track, servants' quarters, and a classical pool complex reminiscent of the one built by William Randolph Hearst at San Simeon.

The Rheems were generous in lending their home. They allowed Navy fliers to use their pool while they were training at St. Mary's College during World War II. They also let the Moraga schools' parents club use the grounds for fund-raisers.

As Rheem Manufacturing prospered, Donald Rheem and his brother took turns as chairman of the board. Another brother,

William Kenneth Rheem, also was listed on the board of directors, but took little part in the business.

By 1938, Rheem Manufacturing had plants in Southern California and Texas making galvanized barrels, tanks, hot-water heaters, and stoves. During World War II, the company built ships in Rhode Island, and manufactured aircraft parts in Southern California and munitions in Richmond.

By 1945 the company was operating plants in 20 countries and generating more than $45 million a year.

Back in Moraga, Rheem kept buying property. At one point he owned 1,650 acres in the Moraga-Orinda area.

In 1937 he entered the development business. He bought land at the Orinda Crossroads and built his first commercial center, which included the Orinda Theatre, a bank, offices, and stores.

He then turned his interest to Moraga because he couldn't expand to his liking in Orinda.

He looked to Moraga to carve out the kind of town he wanted, said Evelyn Nosenzo who, with her husband, took care of Rheem during the last year of his life.

He built roads and gave the town a fire station and land for an elementary school.

Rheem Valley, 1935—the way that most of the central and eastern parts of Contra Costa County looked before the Second World War.

"The development program of Don Rheem was different than most," James Dalton told members of the Moraga Historical Society on Nov. 14, 1968. "He opened a shopping center in what was the middle of a cow pasture without any customers immediately adjoining. His feeling was that if you first create a shopping area, housing will naturally follow. And follow it did," said Dalton, who managed the Rheem California Land Co.

Rheem and his brother Richard lost control of Rheem Manufacturing in the 1960s through an unfriendly takeover. But the two remained in the development business until 1972 with their Rheem California Land Co.

Rheem planned to call his new complex the Moraga Center. Signs were made and installed, said Nosenzo. But town residents protested. They claimed that the historical center was two miles south of Rheem's construction.

Rheem discovered that he could fit his own name on the sign since it had five letters, while "Moraga" had six. He was able to get the postoffice to open a substation at the shopping center with a zip code for Rheem because he used the station for his Richmond business interests.

Rheem's pet project in the center was the theater. Before it opened, on June 12, 1957, he spent $750,000 on it. "Every seat a loge," read the newspaper advertisement for the theater's movies. Rheem's wife died of cancer the year before the theater opened. Five years later he put his Moraga estate up for sale.

Peculiarly, even though he had lavished money, time, and attention on his buildings, he didn't seem to care what happened to them after he was through with them.

"What do they want with that white elephant?" he said when he discovered that the Christian Brothers wanted to buy his Moraga estate, according to Brother Dennis Goodman, St. Mary's College archivist and Moraga historian. The order later sold the estate to the Town of Moraga. When someone told him that the Orinda Theatre he built might be demolished, he reportedly commented, "That's progress."

In December 1982 Rheem had a stroke, and died the following January.

Trees, to Boards, to Ashes

IT WAS 9:30 TUESDAY NIGHT, August 26, 1913, when A. L. Hook brought the Oakland & Antioch Electric Railway train to a standstill at Bay Point (Port Chicago.)

The northern sky above the mammoth C. A. Smith Lumber Yards turned orange-red. Flames leaped high into the air. Hook yanked as hard as he could on the train whistle, alerting the Bay Point employees that their livelihood was about to go up in smoke.

A watchman activated the great siren at the mills, calling workers back to the plant to fight the blaze. The fire, which had started in a dry pile of spruce lumber on the west side of the yard, was spreading with the help of a strong southerly wind.

Plant superintendent Dan C. Desmond rushed to the plant in his automobile to take charge of the battle.

"Calls for help were dispatched to Concord, Richmond, Martinez, Pittsburg, and Antioch. A special train over the Oakland & Antioch Electric, carrying fire-fighters and their hose from Pittsburg, arrived about midnight; a special over the Santa Fe from Richmond also arrived about midnight; and about 1 a.m. the fire tug *Crolona* of the California & Hawaiian Sugar Company was brought out and did valiant service in saving docks and wharves," reported the *Contra Costa Gazette*.

In a desperate effort to stop the fire from reaching the mill and the adjacent box factory, Desmond decided to use dynamite to blow up stacks of lumbers. County Supervisor Vincent Hook of Concord brought the dynamite to the scene himself. Crews led by Constable Charley Palmer placed the dynamite in strategic locations. The tactic didn't work.

Desmond gave the order to start a backfire to burn thousands more feet of cedar, pine, and spruce worth $50 per thousand feet. The mill and box factory were saved. It took 1,000 firefighters to control the flames that night. By the time it was over, 40 million feet of lumber had been destroyed.

Stacks of lumber as far as the eye could see at the C. A. Smith Lumber Yards in Bay Point burned in 1913. It was the biggest fire the county had ever seen.

The cleanup and reconstruction started the next day.

"Nearly all of the yard men assisted by several score of laborers are busily engaged in the fire swept yards of the Smith Lumber Co. at Bay Point rebuilding the (rail) lines, which gridiron the yard and which make the handling of lumber an easy and rapidly performed task.

"That portion of the yard established on marshland which was swept by the flames is now smooth and the ground is as level as a floor and perfectly clean. The suction of the fire and wind carried away every bit of ash and only the twisted rails remain to be carried away," reported the *Gazette* on August 28, 1913.

On September 26, 1913, a month after the fire, the steamer *Adeline Smith* arrived from Coos Bay with the first load of 2 million feet of lumber to get the mill going again.

It wasn't the first time that C. A. Smith had been burned out. In 1892 he lost his first mill in a fire in Minnesota six weeks after he bought it. But he rebuilt it and kept it going just as he would the Bay Point mill.

By the time of the Bay Point fire, Smith owned mills in Minnesota, Oregon, and California. He had a tract of redwoods in Humboldt County, sugar and western yellow pine forests in El

Dorado County and a huge acreage of timber in southwestern Oregon.

He had come to the Bay Area in 1907, looking for a manufacturing site to finish the lumber from his Coos Bay, Oregon mill.

He needed three things—deep water for the ships that would be bringing down the timber from Oregon; dry weather to cure the green timber; and rail connections to ship out the finished product.

Smith heard about the south shore of Suisun Bay, just 40 miles from San Francisco. Bay Point wasn't much of a place. It was mostly tule bogs. But it did have a warehouse, a saloon, a post office, a grocery, and an empty copper smelter. The Copper King Smelting Company, which invested $1.3 million in a smelter and dock, went bankrupt in 1903.

Previous failures didn't bother Smith. He bought 1,500 acres on the shore with deep water, the Southern Pacific and Santa Fe railroads, and dry weather.

He controlled his business from the tree to the final product. He built his own steamers to transport the lumber. It was such an efficient operation that it only took five days to load 2 million feet of lumber in Coos Bay, travel the 850 miles to Bay Point, and unload.

The *Concord Transcript* described the operation in its June 14, 1911 issue.

"The C. A. Smith Lumber Company shipped over 280 cars of lumber, or ten trains of 28 cars each, from here last month. This does not include any shipments from the box factory. How is this for a town that was a barren field three years ago?"

Smith was interested in more than a modern mill. The Swedish immigrant wanted a model, sober town.

He inserted a clause in the deeds of all the lots he sold in Bay Point. The sale of liquor was prohibited. Townspeople didn't pay attention. Soon the less law-abiding were selling liquor out of their back rooms.

After nine years of the experiment, Smith gave up. He allowed the townspeople to put up a saloon on company land. It was a municipally-owned liquor business. All the profits went to town improvements.

Four years after the fire, Bay Point was bigger than either Concord or Walnut Creek. Its population of 1,000 enjoyed cement sidewalks and curbs, a municipal water system, and a sewer system. There were two churches, a school, a drugstore, a hardware store, and several groceries. It seemed as if the town could only grow bigger as the years went by.

Then in 1918 came the biggest boost the little town would ever get. The Pacific Coast Shipbuilding Company built its shipyard next to the lumber mill to provide freighters for World War I. Almost overnight there were close to four thousand people working in Bay Point.

But soon after the end of the war, the shipyard closed down. The lumber mill was sold to Coos Bay Lumber, which cut back operations. In 1940 the lumber company closed operations in Bay Point (now Port Chicago) and moved into Oakland.

Oh, the Wells Fargo Wagon

HENRY WELLS AND WILLIAM FARGO had never been to California when they organized an express company in 1852 to serve the burgeoning, bustling boom towns of the newest state in the Union.

The two, who already had founded the American Express Co. in the East, realized that there was a market in the West waiting to be tapped. They knew that thousands of gold prospectors, more than anything else, wanted letters and packages from home in their remote mining towns. In addition, once their gold was dug, they wanted a safe way to transport it and exchange it for coin. Express companies were not just going to pick up and deliver. Express companies would become the bankers of the Gold Country.

Up to the arrival of express companies, mail service to the mines had been haphazard.

Most of the time the United States postal service didn't have the vaguest idea of where to find such communities as Growlersburg or Ground Hog's Glory, much less find a particular person in those places.

There were enterprising men, such as Alexander H. Todd. Todd would go from mining camp to mining camp and charge miners a dollar to put their names on a list. Todd would take the list to San Francisco, have himself sworn in as a postal clerk, and pick up the mail for the names on the list for delivery to the camps. In addition to the letters, Todd would buy all the New York papers he could lay his hands on. Then, upon returning to the gold fields, he would charge an ounce of gold dust apiece for each letter he delivered and up to $8 for each copy of a newspaper.

The San Francisco postmaster was glad to get rid of the burden of delivering to the mining camps. However, within a short period of time he realized that he too could tap into some of this wealth going to men like Todd, and he began to charge them 25 cents for every letter they picked up.

Within a few months the Todd & Co. Express would have a string of offices. Others also got into the business, including Elliott's Accommodation Express, Reynolds and Co., Gregory and Company's Express, and Adams and Co.

Wells, Fargo and Co. would not be the first express company to enter the California market, but within three years it would be the most financially sound and the biggest.

The first announcement of Wells, Fargo and Co.'s entrance into the express business in California came in the May 20 issue of the *New York Times.*

Samuel Carter, who had been with the American Express, and R. W. Washburn of the Bank of Syracuse, were sent to San Francisco to be Wells, Fargo and Co.'s principal agents. Carter would handle the express business and Washburn the banking. Even before Carter and Washburn arrived to open the first Wells, Fargo and Co. office in San Francisco, the newspaper *Alta California* reported:

"Wells, Fargo & Co.'s Atlantic and Pacific Express, a joint stock company . . . is now ready to undertake a general Express Forwarding Agency and Commission Business; the purchase and sale of Gold dust, Bullion and Bills of Exchange; the payment and collection of Notes, Bills and Accounts; the forwarding of Gold Dust, Bullion and Specie; also, Packages, Parcels and Freight of all descriptions, and between the city of New York and the city of San Francisco, and the principal cities and towns in California."

The office in San Francisco opened on Montgomery Street in July. By August there were three Wells, Fargo and Co. offices in Placer County and four other offices in Sacramento, Benicia, Monterey, and San Diego.

By the end of the year the 47-year-old Henry Wells decided he had to go see what was going on with his new business in California. He left in February, taking the Panama route. It wasn't a pleasant trip and he would never make another one.

He wrote back home to New York: "Thank God the Isthmus is passed and I am alive and kicking but awful sore and tired. It was a dangerous and difficult trip."

While Wells didn't like the journey to California, he liked what he saw when he got here. The San Francisco office was located in a red brick building built by the Mormon Sam Brannan. It already had the green shutters in place, which were to be a hallmark of all the Wells, Fargo offices throughout the country. There was a long line of brass balance scales weighing gold dust to the fraction of an ounce. Profits were growing daily.

Wells's biggest competitors, Page, Bacon & Co. and Adams and Co., were across the street in a stone building on the northwest corner of Montgomery and California streets. That location proved to be a lucky break for Wells, Fargo and Co.

The stones for the building had been imported from China and had been hand cut and numbered in Chinese. When the Chinese masons came to put the building together and found that it was to go on the northwest corner, they refused to work. They contended that evil spirits would inhabit the building. The

Wells Fargo agent William Biglow, in his Antioch office.

contractor managed to put the building together without the help of Chinese masons, but then all the Chinese customers refused to enter the building and instead brought their considerable business to Wells, Fargo and Co. across the street.

Wells was to enthusiastically write: "This is a great Country & a greater people. Our Express is just in from Sacramento & the mines & our Way-bill for New York will amount to nearly $3,000. The amt. going forward by this Steamer as you will see is the largest ever shipped from this Port. Had the express got in from the Southern mines we should have had some Two Hundred Ounces more to add to our amount. But it will come next time."

Concord and Black Bart

THE WELLS, FARGO & CO. express coach was winding its way from Sonora to Calaveras County on July 26, 1875 when a masked man came out of nowhere waving a shotgun.

"Throw down the box," ordered the gunman.

A woman passenger, scared to death, threw her purse at the gunman's feet. He handed it back to her, saying politely he wasn't interested in anyone's money except Wells, Fargo's.

In December of the same year a lone gunman held up a Wells, Fargo stagecoach between Marysville and North San Juan. Then a year later the coach from Yreka to Roseburg, Oregon was held up by a single man.

No one seemed to realize that these robberies were the work of one man until 1877, when the bandit left something behind.

Wells, Fargo stage coaches had been the target of so many holdups that in 1873 the company hired James B. Hume, who had been the marshal of Placerville, the sheriff of El Dorado County, and the warden of the Nevada state prison.

Hume, 6 feet and 1 inch tall, was a powerful man of 200 pounds. Police officials were more than happy to help Hume because he always saw that any rewards went to the local law officers. A bachelor until he was 59, Hume made his home in Oakland where he tended his rose garden in off hours.

Black Bart, the Po8

On August 3, 1877 the Wells, Fargo stage coach traveling from Point Arena south through Sonoma County was held up by a gunman dressed in a long white linen duster with a flour sack on his head.

It wasn't until the next day that police discovered the wrecked express box in a clump of weeds not far from the road. The $300 in coins and a check for $205.32 were missing. But inside the box was a poem.

I've labored long and hard for bread,
    For honor and for riches--
But on my corns too long you've trod,
    You fine-haired sons of bitches.

It was signed Black Bart, the Po8. He probably took the name from a popular mystery serial of the times.

Hume and his aides discovered that after the robbery a middle-aged man showed up in Guerneville, a few miles from where the robbery had taken place. The man had brown hair and beard sprinkled with gray. His eyes were blue and he had a deep voice. The stranger had breakfast and then took a stage out of town.

Ten months later the poetical bandit struck Wells, Fargo again. On June 25, 1878 a gunman in a linen duster with a flour sack over his head stopped the stage running from Quincy to Oroville. He leveled his double-barreled shotgun at the driver and demanded the express mail and the mail bag.

The express box was found the next day. This time the thief got $379 in coin, a $200 diamond ring, and a $25 silver watch. When the police looked into the box they found the original verse plus two additional stanzas.

here I lay me down to sleep
    to wait the coming morrow.
perhaps success, perhaps defeat
    And everlasting sorrow.
let come what will, I'll try it on
    My condition can't be worse
And if there's money in that box
    'Tis munny in my purse.

Black Bart, the Po8, again took credit for the rhyme. Hume always questioned the people who lived close to where the hold-ups had occurred. He determined that Black Bart never used a horse to make his get-away. He was a robber who simply walked away from his deeds.

He acted like a preacher

In October of 1878 Hume got a lucky break. Black Bart had held up two stages in the Ukiah area. The bandit, assuming the

Black Bart didn't look like a holdup man.

role of a tourist, stopped at the McCreary farm near the Eel River, where the 16-year-old daughter waited on him at the breakfast table. She didn't miss a thing.

She gave Hume the best description yet of his quarry, a man of medium height, graying brown hair and beard, deep-set light-blue eyes, heavy brows, no odor of tobacco on his clothing, and his conversation was free from vulgarities. The McCreary family thought he must have been a preacher.

Black Bart had successfully held up Wells, Fargo stages 27 times when on Nov. 3, 1883 he stopped a stage near the spot of his first holdup in 1875. It was to be his biggest haul ever—$4,100 worth of gold amalgam, 3.25 ounces of gold dust, and $553 in gold coin.

The stage had one passenger, a young teenager who had gotten off earlier to walk to Copperopolis in order to hunt for game. When the teenager looked back and spotted Black Bart holding up the stage, he crept around to the driver and handed him his rifle. Black Bart was concentrating on the express box. The driver shot at Black Bart and missed. Black Bart scampered into the brush. But he left behind his Derby hat, a field-glass case, a pair of detachable cuffs, and a handkerchief with the laundry mark "FX07."

Hume went to 90 laundries in San Francisco—and found his man. The handkerchief belonged to Charles Bolton, who claimed he was a mine owner. Bolton was a Civil War veteran who had left his wife and family in Illinois. He also used the names T. Z. Spaulding and Charles E. Boles. While Bolton carried a shotgun, it turned out that he rarely loaded it. He confessed to his crimes and was sentenced to six years in San Quentin. He was released early in 1888 and dropped from sight.

Not quite 100 years later, the Concord Chamber of Commerce made a connection between Charles Boles, a one-time Concord teacher, and Black Bart, claiming that the two were one and the same. Concord gleefully celebrated Black Bart Days to commemorate the opening of BART (Bay Area Rapid Transit). Historians have looked at the record of Black Bart, and never have been able to prove that the poet ever taught school.

Moraga's Wild West

MORAGA may never have turned into a battleground in 1871 if Joaquin Moraga had learned how to read or if Horace W. Carpentier had followed in his father's footsteps and become a cobbler.

Reading and writing weren't high priorities for Moraga. The ex-soldier knew enough to acquire the 13,300-acre Rancho de los Palos Colorados with his cousin Juan Bernal. The problem was that the two didn't know enough to keep it—and neither did their children. Carpentier was too bright to be a shoemaker. A Columbia University graduate, he decided to come to California before opening a law practice.

Like most newcomers to the state, Carpentier went into the gold country. But by mid-1849 he had given up mining and was on a sloop heading down the Sacramento river to San Francisco where he would find real wealth manipulating the law.

The Treaty of Guadalupe Hidalgo between the United States and Mexico was supposed to protect the land grants of Mexican army veterans like Moraga and Bernal. However, Congress effectively changed the purpose of the treaty with a new law. Instead of the United States government having to prove that a Mexican land grant was fraudulent, it was up to the rancho owner to prove the legality of his title. This new law was to prove a bonanza for attorneys such as Carpentier and disaster for unsophisticated ranchers as Moraga and Bernal.

The rancho owners were always short of cash. Moraga and Bernal started selling chunks of their rancho even before their title was settled under American law. Five hundred acres of prime redwood land went to Elam Brown of Lafayette in 1853. Two years later, 40 acres went to Isaac Gann. One time, six acres were signed away to pay off a $90.22 grocery bill.

The Bernal family mortgaged its share of the rancho several times, once paying astronomical rates of interest of 7 and 7½ percent a month. In order to pay attorneys' fees, the widow

Horace W. Carpentier, who discovered that the real gold
was in owning land—and that acquiring the land was
easier than digging for gold.

Bernal gave up a piece of land 1.4 miles wide that extended from modern Orinda to Burton Valley in Lafayette.

Between them, the Moragas and the Bernals had signed away their rancho on dozens of slips of paper.

By the time Carpentier noticed Moraga's holdings, he already had wrested land from the Peralta family holdings to create the city of Oakland, keeping for himself title to the Oakland waterfront, where he collected fees for 37 years.

The *Oakland Daily Transcript* reported in 1877, "Had the early settlers of Oakland taken Horace Carpentier to a convenient tree and hanged him as they frequently tried to do, the act would have been an inestimable and beneficial gift to immediate posterity."

The Moraga and Bernal families' finances were in bad shape even before Carpentier took notice of them, but at least no one was shooting at them.

Carpentier started acquiring the Moraga rancho in 1850 when he bought up a note signed by the Widow Bernal, through which he claimed half of the entire rancho.

He then started eviction proceedings against people who had bought land from Bernal and Moraga in good faith.

Some were scared off. Some paid Carpentier. But Jesse Williams, who paid $5 an acre for his farm in what eventually became the Rheem Valley area, wasn't one of them. He wasn't going to let any fancy New York-educated, land-grabbing attorney swindle him out of his 160 acres.

According to the story told around the community of Moraga, one dark night on Moraga Road Williams met Carpentier. Pointing his gun at Carpentier, Williams forced the attorney to sign a quit claim relinquishing all interest in the 160 acres.

While there is no proof that this actually happened, Williams was the only settler who never had to pay Carpentier for the privilege of staying on his own land.

The shooting started when Isaac Yoakum came on to the scene. Yoakum was a former squatter who decided if he couldn't fight Carpentier, he would join him.

Yoakum in partnership with Carpentier bought one of the Moraga family's notes in 1864, which had mortgaged the last four square miles of the rancho including the family adobe. In January of 1871 Yoakum got a writ of possession to what was left of the Moraga rancho.

The Moragas fought back in court, pointing out that some of the children's names were left off the court order. The sheriff then refused to enforce the claim.

Yoakum, tiring of legal procedures, built a barricade and pitched a tent behind it. Lying in wait with his crew of toughs just beyond the gate of the Moragas' corral, he laid siege to the Moragas in their adobe for the next three months.

On April 9, Yoakum's men opened fire on the adobe. The Moragas weren't hurt. A few days later a horse was shot from under a Moraga worker by William Steele, a Yoakum man.

By May the legal papers giving Yoakum the rancho were straightened out and the sheriff was ordered to evict the Moraga family after it removed its personal property from the adobe.

But the battle continued, and on June 30 two Moraga girls helping a shepherd drive Yoakum's sheep from the family's corral were attacked by Yoakum. He struck Gomacinda Moraga with the butt of his rifle two times. The Moragas answered with rifle fire. Yoakum's horse was shot from under him. The shooting continued throughout the next day when Steele shot and killed Silverio Monjas, a Moraga employee.

The *Contra Costa Gazette* reported that a band of armed men went into the valley in support of the Moragas. The sheriff rode in with a posse to prevent the lynching of Yoakum and Steele. Both men were arrested. Yoakum was fined $500 for the attack on Gomacinda. Steele claimed self defense and was acquitted of murder.

Carpentier finally settled with the Moragas by paying them $10,000. In 1912 Carpentier sold the rancho for $1 million to Charles A. Hooper, the man who brought the lumber industry to Pittsburg.

Good Clean Sport

BOXING PROMOTER Sid Hester was running out of time. It was January 31, 1910. Oscar "Battling" Nelson, the lightweight champion of the world had agreed to fight Adolph "Milwaukee Terror" Wolgast on February 22.

The 45-round fight would draw thousands of Bay Area fans. But Hester didn't have any place to put it.

He had thought the baseball field in Alameda would be ideal. The Alameda City Council turned him down. When Hester suggested a site called Ocean View, closer to the beach, the Alameda mayor threatened to call out the entire Alameda police force to prevent the "pugilistic contest" anywhere in his island city.

Hester found a site in Colma. Now all he had to do was to convince San Mateo County officials.

The deal with both fighters had been struck. Nelson, the champion, had been guaranteed $12,000 with an extra $1,000 for expenses. The challenger settled for $3,750.

When reporters asked Nelson if he wanted to change promoters, he said "I have signed to fight with Hester and I will stand pat so long as he is running things. I have never gone back on my word yet and I do not figure to start now. It's Hester's match. I have signed to fight Wolgast and the fight will come off."

This frantic search for a site caught the eye of Richmond saloon owner Pat Dean. On the side Dean promoted boxing matches in the Richmond area. He also refereed boxing matches. But most of all he boosted Richmond.

Richmond had a ballfield called Lang's Park. It was at Point Richmond at the intersection of Washington and Standard avenues between the Standard Oil refinery and the Santa Fe depot. It had been used as a bullfight arena in 1902.

Dean appeared before the Richmond City Council. With a few dollars the ballfield could be turned into an outdoor boxing arena. Bleachers could be built to seat 20,000 people. It could be done in a few weeks.

Richmond would become the boxing capital of the West, maybe the world. Once the fans learned what an ideal site Richmond was for boxing there would be other matches. Perhaps, even the much-touted heavyweight championship battle between Jim Jeffries and Jack Johnson could be fought in Richmond.

Council members became as excited as Dean. They voted immediately to offer Hester a permit for the boxing match and authorized Dean to make a proposal to Hester.

Hester in the meantime was looking at Colma. Colma was only a five cent ride from downtown San Francisco. Then it looked as if San Mateo County officials would turn Hester down too.

On February 6, Dean went to San Francisco and got an audience with the fight promoter.

"Gentlemen I will make any sort of bet that you can reach Richmond from the ferry building in a shorter time than you can get down to Colma. It takes 35 minutes from this city and only 40 minutes from the center of Oakland.

"I can arrange with the railroad company for a very reasonable rate on the day of the battle and I can also arrange it so the big crowd can be handled with quickness and dispatch. It will demonstrate that Richmond is far superior than either Colma or Alameda. All I want is a good chance to make good," said Dean.

Hester later told reporters that the Point Richmond offer came as a complete surprise. He had his doubts about the location. The ferry boat ride alone would cost 35 cents. However the *San Francisco Chronicle* reported that of all the sites, the Point Richmond one seemed to be the one that would succeed.

On February 7, Hester accepted Dean's proposal.

The three-tiered headline in the *Daily Gazette* in Martinez boasted "Pat Dean Lands Pugilistic Event—Nelson Wolgast Fight Scheduled to Take Place in Richmond. Date Not Fixed."

The story, with a San Francisco dateline, went on to say, "The Nelson-Wolgast fight is to be fought in Richmond on Washington's birthday if Sid Hester is to promote it. This was agreed on last night and incidently it was the only agreement reached."

Hester met with the fight managers to work out the details of the fight. Nelson had recently hired John R. Robinson. Tom Jones

Oscar "Battling" Nelson autographed this photo for Richmond
promoter Pat Dean eight months after the famous lightweight
world boxing championship in Richmond in 1910.

was Wolgast's manager. The meeting was public and drew quite a number of onlookers.

The men could not agree on a referee. Names of referees from Chicago and Philadelphia were tossed about. Tom Jones's stubborness about the choice of the referee got him labeled as a "disturbing element" by some members of the press. Hester said the referee had to be a local official.

The boxers and their managers also argued about a motion picture rights. The Nelson backers had arranged for movies to be taken and were not about to share any of the profits with the Wolgast group.

The meeting was so rancorous that Nelson was moved again to assure the press that the fight would go on.

"I have never gone back on my word yet and I do not figure to start now. It's Hester's match. I have signed to fight Wolgast and the fight will come off if the other fellow is reasonable and we can settle the details without further waste of time. Richmond looks good to me. It's the best of the lot," said Nelson.

Dean promised reporters:

"We will start in on the arena immediately. It will only take a few days to fit out the ballpark to accommodate up to 20,000 people and I believe at least 15,000 will be on hand to witness the big battle. I am willing to gamble right now that Richmond will contribute 3,000 (fans)."

On February 9 a shipload of lumber arrived at the ballfield— some 200,000 board feet. G. A. Follett, a city councilman as well as a building contractor, was in charge of the building project.

Follett hired an army of carpenters. He had less than two weeks to finish the job.

"A Bloody, Brutal Exhibition"

PAT DEAN reveled in all the attention the upcoming world championship brought to him and to Point Richmond.

His saloon, with its stained glass windows proclaiming "Yosemite Lager," appeared on postcards sold as souvenirs of the fight. He posed at the end of his long shiny bar wearing his derby hat and chomping on a black cigar. Fight promoter Sid Hester left all the decisions regarding the building of the arena to Dean. Newspaper reporters labeled the Richmond saloon owner "a prominent sport," and called him one of the most influential businessmen in Contra Costa County.

G. A. Follett, Richmond council member and a building contractor was in charge of building spectator bleachers and the boxing ring. The boxers got into a dispute over the size of the ring. Nelson wanted a 23-foot ring. Wolgast insisted on a smaller one.

On February 17, the *Contra Costa Gazette* reprinted excerpts from the *San Francisco Call* written by columnist William Slattery under the headline "Eyes of Fans Turn to Richmond."

"If the sun shines brightly over in Richmond next Thursday afternoon a record throng will jam the spacious arena to watch Bat Nelson and Ad Wolgast maul each other around the ring for the lightweight championship of the world.

"Every section of the state will send its delegation and Richmond will become famous throughout the length and breadth of California. There is nothing like a fight to stir a man's interest. There will be many a man at the ringside who has never witnessed a Marquis of Queensbury struggle before. But it all depends on the weather."

Hester was taking a chance with an outdoor arena. There wouldn't be a tent covering the ring, and Hester had decided that insuring the event with Lloyds of London for $3,000 against rain would be too expensive. He based his hopes on the fact that for the past six years there had been dry, fair weather on February 22.

The fighters didn't care if it rained or not. Hester had signed a contract assuring they would get their money no matter how many people showed up.

The oddmakers favored Nelson in the bout, giving him 10 to 7 odds. On February 19, tickets went on sale at Kelly's Cigar Store in Martinez. Reserve seats ranged from $3 to $15. Sales were brisk.

Nelson arranged for a side bet of $5,000 on himself. On February 19 Nelson's weight was reported at 133 and Wolgast's at 131. The press criticized Nelson for his lack of serious training.

Nelson responded, "I think this fellow Wolgast is a big boob who has no punch that will hurt me."

On the morning of February 22 a big rain storm blew over Richmond. The dirt roads turned into mud. But the weather didn't stop any fans. By fight time the rain stopped. The stands filled up by 2 p.m. A cold wind blew in on the arena from the Bay.

Wolgast was the first of the two fighters to arrive at the arena, at 2:54 p.m. He was kept waiting for 15 minutes while Nelson, wearing a red flannel shirt over his trunks, was carried through the crowd on the shoulders of his aide, Abdul the Turk.

Wolgast was heard to mutter, "It will be the last time he'll ever be carried anywhere as a champion."

Shortly after 3 p.m. the fight began. It had been scheduled for 45 rounds. The referee, Eddie Smith from Oakland, stopped the fight in the 40th round, raising the gloved hand of Wolgast and declaring him the winner. The fight took three hours.

"A bloody, brutal exhibition," reported the *Gazette*.

"For ten rounds it looked as if Nelson might save his laurels. He was the aggressor and at times the fight looked something like a foot race around the area. Wolgast pursued and Nelson pursuing.

"Now and again Wolgast would stand his ground and almost invariably landed telling body blows and fierce uppercuts.

"Nelson was soon bleeding freely from nose, lips, and left ear. So much gore flowed from him that when engaged in close in fighting Wolgast's neck and shoulders became profusely bespattered with Nelson's blood."

The *San Francisco Chronicle* called Wolgast a shrewd hard-headed fighter and reported that Nelson didn't have the speed.

Fifteen thousand fans showed up at the Point Richmond battle. Fight receipts totaled $37,000. Nelson collected $12,000, but then had to pay off his side bet of $5,000. Wolgast got $3,750.

February 22, 1910, the last round. "Battling" Nelson, at the left, is beaten by "Milwaukee Menace" Wolgast.

The next day Wolgast was beseiged by offers. He said he might take off a year from the fighting game and go on the stage. His manager had different ideas. He said his fighter would accept any reasonable challenge.

Joe Gans, a black American lightweight, challenged him to a fight. Wolgast's manager, Tom Jones said the challenge "would not be given any notice. My fighter will not fight a colored man."

Nelson, barely able to talk, announced he was opening a theatrical engagement in Chicago and negotiating for a $10,000 fight with "Cyclone" Johnny Johnson.

Education? Who Needs It?

WHEN William Penniman read the notice tacked on the front of the Pleasant Hill school house that September day in 1891 it made him hopping mad.

There was going to be an election to create a union high school district, and he didn't know a thing about it. The fact that he was the clerk of the Pleasant Hill School Board of Trustees made him all the angrier. If anyone should have known what was going on, he should have.

Central Contra Costa students had gotten along fine without a high school ever since the county was created 40 years earlier—so thought Penniman.

Someone was trying to pull a fast one, he wrote in his letter to the *Contra Costa Gazette* published on Sept. 26, 1891.

"In what way is this proposition sprung upon us? The first inkling we have of it is in the shape of bills or notices . . . notifying the electors of the Pleasant Hill School district that an election will be held at the school house on a certain day to vote for or against a high school."

At the time Penniman wrote his letter, less than six per cent of the students in California ever went to high school. Penniman was among the majority who felt that eight years of free education was adequate, and if anyone wanted more than that they should be willing to pay for it themselves and not burden the taxpayer.

He thought it grossly unfair that a majority of votes in other elementary school districts could force an unwilling Pleasant Hill district to pay for a union high school.

"In the districts having a majority vote for the high school, it is no more than just that they should support the school, but confine its support there and not go into districts opposed to the Union High School District."

The reason for the push to start high schools in 1891 was that the state legislature passed a law allowing elementary school districts to join together to create a union high school district. However, as usual, the legislature didn't provide any money for the new schools.

As was to be expected, a big problem the law created was where to put a high school. Antioch, which had experimented with high school classes in its elementary school building in 1883, wanted the high school for east Contra Costa children. People in Brentwood and Byron didn't want to pay for a school that far away.

Walnut Creek proposed that it be the site of the high school for central county students. Penniman thundered that Walnut Creek would be too hard to get to for Pleasant Hill students.

"The people in our district nearly all say (that is, those who have children) that a high school at Walnut Creek would not benefit them, as it is too far for their children to drive morning and evening and study besides, and if they would have to pay their board they would much rather send them to a better institution."

"If people want the best education to be had in this state or perhaps any other, why do they not send their children to the Leland Stanford, Jr. University, where a far superior education can be had for less than it would cost to send them to Walnut Creek High School, except perhaps those who live in that town."

Penniman went on to say that most of the people were too poor to be able to afford to send their children to high school. According to Penniman, the parents wanted their children out on their own—earning a living before they turned "twenty-three or twenty-four years."

Penniman had his critics, and after the election failed, one of them answered Penniman, signing his letter, "A Lover of Education."

The Lover of Education pointed out that Penniman had 10 days following the posting of the election notice to educate himself about the issues, which was more than enough time: "If he did not do so, it is not our fault."

Penniman also was criticized for opposing the very small amount it took to support a union high school.

"Don't be selfish. If you have no children of your own to

educate, try to help your neighbor who has children. . . . Selfishness belongs to Europe.

"It appears to me there is nothing we need more than good schools, and especially the high school.

"Now then, let me ask my noble friend (Penniman) what it is that has placed our government above all other governments, for the best form of government. It is our free school system, placing the poorer classes upon an even plane with the richer classes in education, making the rich pay for the poor, thereby creating equal rights and privileges for all. This is what our free primary schools have done in the last 50 years.

"All I have got to say is will you stop kicking against a high school tax, and read and try to understand our high school system?"

The letter from the Lover of Education made Penniman all the angrier. Even though the union high school issue had failed locally for the time being it didn't stop Penniman from writing another letter to the editor.

Mt. Diablo Union High School in 1901—on the same site in Concord where it is today.

"Walnut Creek, Oct. 15, 1891

"Ed. Gazette:—I would state that this great "Lover of Education" has attacked me in such an ungentlmany (*sic*) way that as a gentleman myself I shall not notice his slurs on my education, but if he would like to see my deploma (*sic*) he can come to my home and I will gladly show it to him."

Penniman explained that he represented some of the biggest taxpayers in his district when he complained about the tax for the new high school.

"For myself I do not mind the extra tax if it is going to benefit the community at large, but when (Pleasant Hill) people say that they would not patronize the school, what is the use of our paying heavy taxes and receiving no benefit.

"I think if that town (Walnut Creek) wants a high school it should have one, but it should not expect outside help unless given voluntarily."

While Central County residents failed in their attempt to get a high school in 1891, the residents of East County established a high school on the second floor of the Antioch Grammar School Building. Students came from as far west as Bay Point (Port Chicago) and what is now West Pittsburg, and as far east as Byron.

The school continued for four years, but without state financing it failed, and was closed down in 1895 when the furniture was sold.

In 1901 the state legislature decreed that state financing for free high schools would begin in 1903. With this new law, union high school districts were then created in Martinez (Alhambra), Concord (Mt. Diablo), Antioch (Riverview), San Ramon and Liberty (Brentwood.)

The March of Progress

Benicia folks pulled out all the stops on April 16, 1878. It was time to celebrate. The city across from Martinez on the Carquinez Strait had just been connected to the rest of the continent by virtue of the Northern Railway link to Suisun and Fairfield.

The neighborly Martinez Brass Band crossed the strait by ferry to ride on the excursion train.

"Benicia was gay with bunting at an early hour in the morning, and at about ten o'clock a train of three passenger coaches and a flat car carrying a piece of brass artillery and the Martinez Band, started out from First Street with booming salutes and stirring music, drawn by Engine No. 5, beautifully decked with flags and festoons, bouquets and wreaths of flowers," reported the *Contra Costa Gazette*.

On the way to Suisun the train stopped at the Benicia Military Post to pick up the commander and other passengers. Some 200 people made the hour-long trip. It was a relatively smooth ride, with the cars gently oscillating from side to side as the train reached speeds of more than 20 miles an hour.

Suisun residents had decorated their city hall with flags and streamers. After speeches of welcome from both Suisun and Fairfield officials, Suisun hosted their guests to lunch and a dance at the Roberts House.

At 3 p.m. the Benicia passengers boarded the train and headed for home. Benicia officials held a meeting in one of the passenger cars and adopted a series of resolutions declaring the importance of the enterprise and thanking and congratulating the directors and builders of railroad, the people of Suisun and Fairfield and the Martinez Brass Band.

A Missing Piece

With the completion of the Benicia to Suisun connection to the California Pacific line, the railroad builders now had most of their Bay Area routes in place. But there was still a vital piece of the operation missing. And that was how to get their overland trains across the Carquinez Strait to complete the journey.

It is true that there was a long, looping route from Sacramento to Oakland via Tracy and Niles Canyon. But the railroad men had something else in mind. If they could somehow make a crossing at the Carquinez Strait they could save 62 miles.

The people of Benicia and Martinez knew that the railroad builders had some sort of crossing in mind back in August 1877 when the company started charting the bottom of the strait to find out how deep it really was.

On September 9, 1877 the editor of the *Contra Costa Gazette* reported:

"The deep water boring float of the Railroad Company has been employed for the past two weeks in testing the substratum character and depth of the bottom on a line from the Pacific Mail Steamship works at Benicia, in the direction of Shepherd Valley, on this side of the Straits, about two miles below Martinez.

"We hear the water averages about 40 feet in depth on the line, with about that average depth of soft mud before reaching any bottom of firm consistency for holding piling. It is said that the examination is being made to determine the practicability or impracticability of bridging the Straits should it be found desirable and admissable."

A Bridge Across The Strait?

Conservative thinkers shrugged at the thought of a bridge. With a population of 12,000, more or less, in Contra Costa it didn't seem that profitable. The railroad kept taking soundings in different areas of the strait, leading the *Gazette* editor to wonder in his issue of January 26, 1878:

"It is presumed the soundings and borings are being made with reference to determining the feasibility of bridging the Straits. But, if even Congress would authorize the construction of a bridge across a navigable arm of the ocean of such importance, it is very questionable if, considering the great cost, the delays to which their trains would be subject for the constant passage of vessels, the liability for their damage and detention by the obstruction, and various other contingencies."

The Southern Pacific ferry *Solano* at Port Costa. Note the "RESTAURANT"
signs at both sides, and the dapper gentleman in white at the left.

Whether the railroad builders were really thinking of a
bridge, and the soundings scared them off, the *Gazette* never
reported, because it soon became clear that there was something
else in the wind.

In April the Vallejo newspaper reported the rumor that the
railroad company had bought 150 acres near tunnel number
one (at what eventually became Port Costa) to build a terminal.
Martinez people downplayed this report. They hoped that whatever the railroad builders had in mind, it would be in Martinez.

It's A Ferry

The railroad company took soundings throughout the spring
and summer. Then in September the editor scanned the pages of
the *Sacramento Record-Union* and found this interesting item.

"The draftsmen at the railroad works (in Sacramento) are
engaged upon the plans for the machinery of the ferry steamer to
be employed in crossing the trains of the Northern Railway between Benicia and Martinez. She is to be the largest and most
powerful ferry boat ever built, and capable of taking on a large
train of cars and the locomotive."

By then it had been revealed that the railroad company had

bought land for a terminal in Port Costa, which was to be the site of the ferry crossing. Martinez would continue to be served by local trains, but it would no longer be on the great transcontinental route. Once the ferry began to operate, transcontinental trains would cross the Carquinez Strait before they came to Martinez.

In January 1879 the readers of the *Gazette* read about the dimensions of this ferry, the *Solano*, which would ply the strait for the next 51 years without a major accident. At the time, it was the largest vessel ever to be built in the United States, some 420 feet long and 117 feet in width.

"Upon the deck of the *Solano* are four tracks extending her entire length, with a capacity for carrying 48 loaded freight cars, or 24 passenger coaches of the largest class. The pilot houses are elevated over 40 feet above the main deck and afford the helmsman a clear view fore and aft of the boat."

Construction on the giant ferry slips on both sides of the strait started in January. The ferry boat, which was built in Oakland, made a trial run across the strait on November 25. After a month of trials, the ferry hauled its first train on December 28.

There was little fanfare in the *Gazette*—nothing like the article it printed when service started in Benicia. The paper issued the new train schedule.

"This change deprives us of the overland trains, but we are to have another local train, making two daily, between San Francisco and Antioch, and the Los Angeles trains remain with us of course," reported the *Gazette*.

A week later there was a bit of sour grapes in the *Gazette* columns:

"Benicia is elated with hope of great improvements to be realized from the new railroad facilities. But the indulgence of too extravagant anticipations may result in great disappointment."

INDEX